NINE MAYAN WOMEN

NINE MAYAN WOMEN

A VILLAGE FACES CHANGE

Mary Elmendorf

SCHENKMAN PUBLISHING COMPANY, INC.

Halsted Press Division
John Wiley and Sons
New York   London   Sydney   Toronto

Copyright © 1976

Schenkman Publishing Company, Inc.
3 Mt. Auburn Place
Cambridge, Massachusetts 02138

Library of Congress Cataloging in Publication Data

Elmendorf, Mary Lindsay.
  Nine Mayan women: a village faces change.

  "A Schenkman publication."
  Bibliography: p.
  1. Women in Chan Kom, Mexico—Case studies.
2. Mayas—Social life and customs. 3. Mayas—
Religion and mythology. I. Title.
HQ1465.C5E45   1976   301.41'2'09726   74-12464
ISBN 0-470-23862-3
ISBN 0-470-23864-X (pbk.)

Printed in the United States of America

Table of Contents

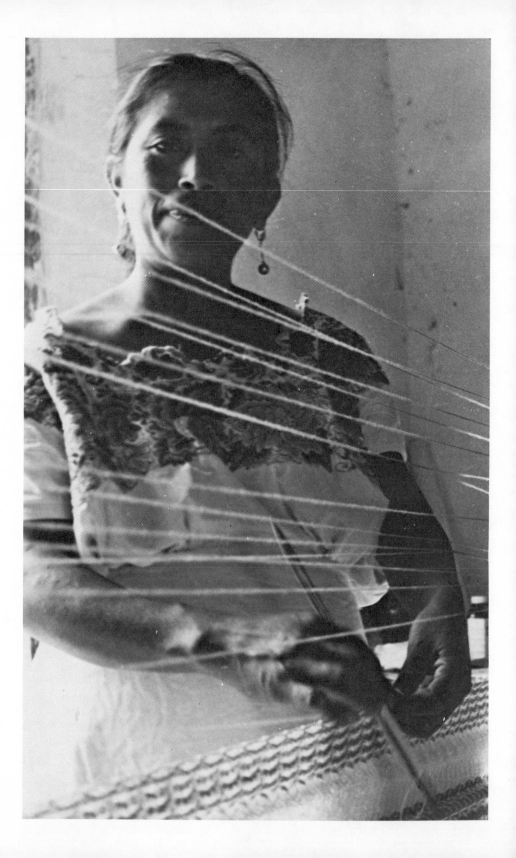

Dedication

To the people of Chan Kom, especially, and with a deep sense of gratitude, to the women. They have shared with me their lives, their hearths, their fears and hopes for the future. This is their story and I have tried my best to keep it that way, changing only personal names to protect their privacy. It is my sincerest wish that a better understanding of these women will help us to understand peasant women in other cultures, and to see them as human resources which must be creatively participating if we are to achieve a better life in our rapidly changing world.

Foreword

It is a matter of deep satisfaction for me to write these brief introductory lines for Dr. Elmendorf's book about the world of Mayan women, both because it involves a worthy contribution to the ethnography of that ethnic group and because of the delicacy and sympathy which she has shown in the handling of such a fascinating theme. Moreover, this book serves to fill a vacuum in the field of Mayan ethnography, since never before has there been a systematic study of this kind; the data which there were about the ways and customs of the female sex had been gathered by ethnographers in the course of general research, and, furthermore, without any opportunity to succeed in getting the depth and spontaneity which characterizes the work which is now put in the reader's hand. Dr. Elmendorf had sufficient patience, understanding and empathy to succeed in gaining the friendship, affection and total confidence of her informants, so that her role as participant-observer always had the approval of the community, which made it easier for her to take advantage of the best opportunities for exchanging confidential impressions with the most representative women in the group; thus, among her informants could be included Luz, more than fifty years old and of high social status, and Felicia, only seventeen and still unmarried. Achieving this kind of rapport resulted in large measure from the fact that the author conducted herself with extreme simplicity and naturalness, as well as sharing the bed and board of her women friends, just as any neighbor there would have done.

Insofar as concerns Chan Kom, the village in which this study was carried out, it is appropriate to recall that it was the place chosen in 1931 by Dr. Robert Redfield in which to begin his now classic study of the process of change which takes place in the behavior of people passing from a rural to an urban society. At the time, I had a chance to take part in the research and to become intimately familiar with the ways of life in the region. In those days, Chan Kom was a remote village, scarcely known by outsiders and inhabited only by Mayan Indians, chained to their language and to the ways of their ancient tradition; these latter were structured to a degree that, using Redfield's terminology, they could be described as "a body of conventional values," which suggested that the way one person understood life had to be the way all did. The *ethos* then existing was characterized by its adherence to work, austerity, sobriety and religious devotion.

Later on, when Dr. Redfield returned in 1948 to examine the changes that had occurred in those seventeen years, it was found that the *ethos* continued to be the same, even to the extent that the same pagan ceremonies for the gods of wind, water and agriculture were being practiced with the same intensity. On the other hand, it was noted that the most obvious changes were the abandoning of the *metate* in favor of the motor-driven mill, the use of metal articles of kitchenware, and the substitution of clothing imported from the city for the traditional garb.

On the social plane, the domestic make-up had stayed the same, although with a certain tendency to relinquish the type of extended household which had been considerably meaningful in the past; the nuptial ceremony had lost much of its normative force, with elopement or simple free union occurring with much greater frequency.

The *fagina,* or free community labor which had contributed so much to the development of the village, had practically disappeared. All these changes, although carried out in a gradual rhythm and without any apparent disruption to established order, were already indicative of the first steps in the modernization process which is observable in other areas of semi-rural people, having among its most conspicuous characteristics the breakdown in the organization of the conventional value system and the rise of individualism and secularization, already pointed out by Redfield in his conceptual scheme.

Twenty-three years later, in December of 1970, the author of these lines had a chance to spend a week in the village and to gather some data about the direction which the above-mentioned process was following. Of course, the most salient point to be observed was that the population had dwindled; indeed, of the 437 who had been there in 1948, now there were 415, distributed among 82 families; of these, 47 were natives of Chan Kom and 35 of various communities in the region, such as Ebtun, Dzitnup, Chikindzonot and from nearby ranches such as Xiatil, Muchukuxcah, and X-Kopteil; furthermore, this figure included a neighbor from Mérida, of Mayan origin who was engaged in bee-keeping. These new people who had arrived from the interior appeared to me to be more rustic and conservative than the Chan Kom natives; in fact, the "colony" of twenty families who had come from Xiatil grouped together on the outskirts of town forming their own *barrio,* recalled the form of living which I had encountered in the jungles of Quintana Roo forty years earlier.

In contrast, the genuine residents of Chan Kom continue to have their sights set on progress, taking as their model the urban type of life, both in their style of dress and in their general conduct; a good number of women had adopted the citified mini-skirt and short curled hair; others were keeping the typical dress, some in the form of a *"mini-huipil."* The use of Spanish was already more wide-spread. As for the men, they were beginning to consider work in the *milpas* non-productive and tiring. For that reason, several had already given it up in order to devote themselves permanently to cattle-raising or commerce, while others had established themselves in Mérida in search of wider horizons. The most enterprising had bought land to begin small cattle ranches. The mercantile spirit had spread even to the women, who were now busying themselves with embroidering native *huipiles* on their sewing machines, or weaving fine hammocks to sell to the tourists at Chichen Itza; two or three of them were making bread and a few others candles for the local market. Among the young men, the most significant thing I noticed was the existence of the three exellent bands, complete with traps and bongos, of the type which frequent the night clubs of Mérida, even including soloists well versed in modern "rock and roll" music. Right then, this activity was not productive enough to permit the players to give up agriculture, although it was presenting enticing prospects, since they were already in demand for fiestas on the Saint's Days of neighboring towns and ranches.

This whole matter of fiestas came to my attention because they are no longer motivated simply by devotion as before, but also by the profit motive, since the substantial sale of beer has become a business from which anyone who can pay the price of a franchise can benefit. Moreover, the dances are no longer free but must be paid for by the men. Family solidarity, although it still exists, no longer has either the cohesion or the spontaneity of before; individualistic tendencies continue to be noticeable and everyone is beginning to think of his personal well-being. This disposition can be clearly appreciated in the words which the husband of Amparo (son of the old leader-creator of Chan Kom) expressed to the author of this book:

During ten years I worked for my father. The only thing which I gained was my sweat. a few times in the *milpa,* or with him on the ranch, or doing other things, if I earned any money I had to give it to him. If there was corn, he would sell it and keep the money. He bought *solares* and land and cattle and put it all in his name and said it was his. He would say that it really belonged to Don Trini and sons, but none of his sons has received anything. He says that we will have it when he dies. But will anything remain? Will we be alive?

This kind of recrimination against the father would have been inconceivable at the time the first study was made in 1931. The growth of the individualistic spirit is being stimulated by the six or eight families which have established themselves in Mérida and which frequently visit the village bringing with them the "advanced" ideologies of urban life.

But nothing exhibits the contrast between the old and the new better than the exceptional experience which I had during my visit in 1970. On that occasion it was possible for me to be present, around midnight, at the pre-hispanic ceremony called *loh-kex,* during which foods are offered to the *yumtzilob* or the masters *(dueños)* of the bush, so they will permit the use of the lands in their charge. This particular case was an attempt to prevent the *yumtzilob* from continuing to punish with sickness certain cattle belonging to a hut recently built on a piece of the mountain. On arriving at the site I sensed the same primitive ambience which I had experienced forty years ago, when the village was just beginning to form: in a clearing in the forest a rustic altar of logs, moss and green branches; at a short distance the *pib* or open oven in the earth for cooking the sacred breads; the *h-men* or shaman arranging the offerings in their proper order, and each in turn, the helpers and guests attending this singular event; to complete the exotic picture, there was no illumination but that of the burning logs from the recently opened oven. Once everything was in its place according to the rules of the ritual, the *h-men,* standing in front of the altar, began the offering of gifts amid prayers and chants in Mayan. All this atmosphere of seclusion and profound communion between man and the supernatural was immediately violated when a group of modern young men, back in the forest, turned on their transistor radio to listen to rock-and-roll music from metropolitan stations. For them, what was happening was nothing but simple diversion and anachronistic remnants of obsolete customs. The experience left me profoundly impressed, and with a certain feeling of sorrow.

Lately these changes have been occurring with greater frequency and are of pronounced significance; principally this can be seen in the asphalt highway which now connects the village with the tourist center of Chichen Itzá and makes it easily accessible to visitors from all over.

In addition, the new bus service has multiplied contacts with the city. The desire to live in a city atmosphere is becoming widespread, as can be seen in the case of Felicia and her sisters as cited by Dr. Elmendorf. It is also important to mention the modernizing influence which the National Indian Institute has systematically had since selecting Chan Kom as a point of disseminating new teachings. They are in the process of developing their own technical staff to teach about agriculture, animal husbandry, medicine and other activities.

The general disposition towards change is now clearly manifest and is decisive to the extent that the Indians themselves are working at it with determination; the author of this book tells us that:

> Mayan women not only accept change, they will initiate or agitate for change—even against their husband's wishes—if it seems best for them and their children. An example of this is their desire for birth control measures.

With this background it should be easy to foresee that the future of Chan Kom has now begun on an irreversible path toward a consumer society which, notwithstanding its many positive aspects, is scarcely propitious for the full enjoyment of a peaceful and harmonious existence.

Dr. Elmendorf, humanist *par excellence,* takes note of the inevitability of change and concerns herself with the dangers and difficulties which wait for these people in the future; this gives her the opportunity to dedicate the last chapters of this exceptional book to considerations of deep philosophic import on what constitutes "the good life," that is to say, on the life-style generated in a more humane society, one in which the members concern themselves not only with efficiency and production, but also with the enjoyment of friendship, of beauty, of knowledge, and of so many other noble things which enrich human experience. This type of existence appears to be rather removed from actual consumer society, and in moving toward it, the natives of Chan Kom will encounter, according to Dr. Elmendorf,

> the pockets of poverty which comprise the *barrios* and the soulless ghettos of the inner city, both in latin America and the United States. In this move out, many experience culture shock, and too often the women suffer most . . . (because) their role is undefined, uncertain and undignified . . .

This book presented by my distinguished colleague permits us to approach very closely the world of the Mayan woman, with its constellations of usages, customs, practices and attitudes toward love, desires and frustrations, reticences and confidences, as manifested in the intimate talks which nine informants had with the author. Independent of this descriptive aspect of warm sincerity, the book offers very serious and timely reflections on the nature of the existence of a changing society like ours, in which optimism and enjoyment of life are becoming marginal. The author gives us her point of view with highly constructive suggestions on regaining this sense of identity and satisfaction, which are becoming so lacking in modern man. We are dealing, then, with a book full of hope and rich in information which, without doubt, will occupy a distinguished place among the studies of peasant women in general.

Alfonso Villa Rojas
Mexico City

Preface

This book is an expanded and enlarged version of a previous work, *La mujer Maya y el cambio,* published in Spanish by the Mexican Ministry of Education and of a limited multilith version by CIDOC. In its present form, it is written for students and members of the public interested in the social sciences in the broadest sense and in the nature of peasant societies in a narrower one. It will be useful for college and university students concerned with the roles of women, the Mayan area, peasant societies in general, and the ways in which traditional peoples make the transition from subsistence to consumer cultures. I began it with the intention of filling what I perceived as a gap in the literature about women, the scarcity of research about the world they live in and the roles they play in peasant societies. Subsequently, I narrowed the scope to focus intensively on Mayan women and finally on the women of Chan Kom, a Mayan village already familiar to students of anthropology.

My interest in the Mayan woman dates back to 1952 when, for the first time, I visited the Tezeltal/Tzotzil zone of the State of Chiapas at the invitation of Dr. Gonzalo Aguirre Beltran, then Director of the first Regional Coordinating Center of the Mexican National Indian Institute. There I met the first Mayan women to be trained by the Institute as village workers. During the nine years that followed this first encounter, and in the course of my work as Chief of the Care Mission to Mexico, I had many further opportunities to recognize and appreciate the potential of women for participation in community development programs in ways which made them more effective and more humane. I saw women of all ages and levels of learning, the illiterates and the professionals, wives of Governors and simple peasants, all contributing to increase the efficiency of the work of many different agencies in all parts of the country.

When in 1961 I returned to the United States, I continued to be concerned with the role of women as under-used human resources in socio-economic development. For the next ten years I worked in many varied projects of a cross-cultural nature associated with the Peace Corps, The Overseas Education Fund, A.I.D. and with student and women's groups. Once again I had an opportunity to share in the hopes, dreams, joys and, sometimes, frustrations of women from many Latin American countries. Each of these experiences reinforced my desire to study in more detail a specific group of women, one which would enable me to explore the nature of their motivations and the way in which they are confronting the world-wide problem of making the transition from a traditional to a modern society. For this purpose I eventually chose Chan Kom, whose women are, in a sense, a symbolic representation of peasant women everywhere.

At this point I began planning for field work in Mexico, and consulted with scholars knowledgeable in and concerned with the several aspects of the problems I planned to attack. With their help, I hoped to complete a conceptual framework for the research, one which could be appropriate for the cross-cultural study of women against the backdrop of various prior ethnographic and community studies. I also wanted to explore the feasibility of using one or more of the questionnaire-type approaches which might give my study more comparative validity. Among those instruments which I initally tested were the questionnaire on Traditionalism and Modernization of the Ethnographic Section of the Mexican Institute of Anthropology and History, the questionnaire which Beverly Chinas used in her research on the Zapotec women of Oaxaca, and the much more comprehensive life history outline recommended by Alfonso Villa Rojas, who encouraged me to do an intensive study of a few women. I took all of these materials with me, together with the revised questionnaire from the Fromm-Maccoby study on *Social Character in a Mexican Village.* This last item I discussed further with Erich Fromm, who pointed out those specific questions which he felt would elicit the most understanding of the role of women as it related to their real role in a life-centered traditional community.

My first field trip to Chan Kom was essentially exploratory in nature, an attempt to gather impressions and preliminary data which could provide me with a basis for evaluating subsequent processes. Since the people of Chan Kom invited me to return, I felt it of utmost importance to speak with Alfonso Villa Rojas, who had done the initial study of Chan Kom with Redfield for the Carnegie Institute. We discussed the current state of affairs in Chan Kom, the relevance of my research plan to other on-going studies, and the tactical and strategic moves I might make to maximize the effectiveness of the project, without in any way harming the integrity of the village.

My personal hopes for the project to some extent transcended what might be called objective analysis and impinged on such questions as quality of life, the nature of the humanistic and phenomenological aspects of peasant women's life, and the sense of harmony with nature which I had so strongly felt on my first visit. I had realized that such questions as, "Are you satisfied with your life?" yielded responses which raised very profound questions about the life-view of these women. In my conversations with both Fromm and Villa Rojas, I sought to clarify some of the key concepts, as much to clear my own mind as to prepare for the field experience.

The detailed description of actual field methods is included in the body of the book. I should note here, however, that I made repeated field trips of varying lengths to Chan Kom between March 1971 and July 1972. These visits were supplemented by extended trips to Mexico City for follow-up research and consultation.

To all the members of the village of Chan Kom, and to the women in particular, I express my deepest gratitude. I am also grateful to the Union Graduate School for the support they gave my project. My special thanks go to Helen Hall Stephens, who made available to me a quiet, beautiful and creative retreat where most of this book was written.

I have, over all these years, accumulated debts of gratitude to many others, both in Mexico and in the United States. In Mexico, I should like to mention especially Gonzalo Aguirre Beltran, Alfonso Villa Rojas, Fernando Camare Barabachano, Erich Fromm, Ivan Illich, and Isabel Kelly. In the United States, I owe a very special debt to the late John Gillin, who first introduced me to anthropology and who, with his wife Helen, early encouraged me to undertake this study. Michael Maccoby, Roy Fairfield, Beverly Chiñas, Sol Tax, Joseph Kahl, and George Foster all contributed suggestions and criticisms which have been of great value. Dorothy Lee in particular, by her example and her exhortations, helped me keep a humanistic and phenomenological approach to my task.

A work of this kind has deep roots in the past. For over thirty years David and Mary McClelland have been close and critical friends, whose support and encouragement helped make this study possible. Evey and David Riesman and Beatrice and John Whiting have also influenced my work and it is the richer for it. A special thanks is also due to Margaret Park Redfield, who remembers and is remembered by the people of Chan Kom, along with her husband the late Robert Redfield.

I would also like to thank my research assistant Mary Hamilton Trimble, who has helped with translations, transcribing tapes, and with the editing. Susan Elmendorf Roberts and William Herman assisted with field work and interviewing in Chan Kom, Patricia Barrand Herman and Ralph Colb helped with the typing. And husbands as well as wives should have special thanks. Without the support and encouragement of my husband, John Elmendorf, I would never had felt free to devote so much time and effort to this book.

What is written here is, in the final analysis, my responsibility. I have had much help and acknowledge it with appreciation, but where I may have written things which grew out of my personal experience of learning—as I have in much of this book— I gladly assume responsibility.

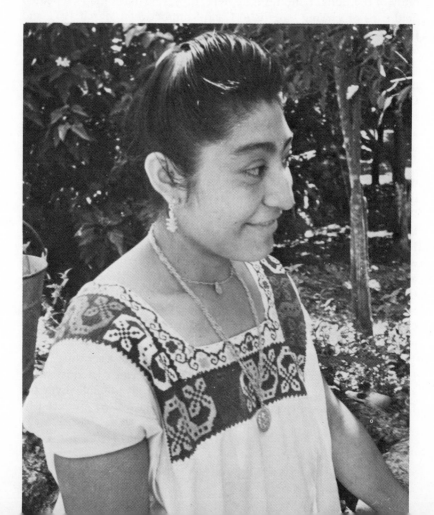

NINE MAYAN WOMEN

Introduction

The Problem

On a recent visit to Mexico, I was told about an interesting problem encountered by directors of a project designed to introduce improved corn into villages in the state of Puebla. Facilities had been arranged which could easily be repaid from the promised doubled yield of the first crop. The peasant farmers appeared enthusiastic at the presentation, but none followed through with the request for a loan. Project officials were very puzzled by this until they finally learned from field workers that the farmers' wives, whom no one had thought to invite to the presentation, controlled the purse strings to a considerable extent and would not permit their husbands to go into debt. As soon as the program was presented and explained to the women, loans were taken out. At this point the project is succeeding quite well.

As we take a new look at this global world, we are increasingly aware of the human element that has been often ignored—the unused human potential. One last human potential to be recognized is the potential of women.

There are more than three billion people in the world. Of these, more than half still live in peasant communities. Of these in turn, over half are women. Thus, the sheer arithmetic of the situation underscores the urgency of knowing more about the life, character, and roles of peasants, including these peasant women. It is to a small portion of this task that the present work addresses itself.

Since historically there have been varying definitions of the terms "peasant," "peasant society," and "peasant life," it is appropriate to clarify them as I have used them in this paper. Fundamentally, I have accepted the conceptual framework of peasant society expounded by Redfield in his short book *Peasant Society and Culture* (Redfield, 1956). The salient feature of peasant society is its universality in both time and space, its specific relationship to the land and the cultivation of the land, and its essentially traditional character. Thus, peasants are those who "have at least this in common: Their agriculture is a livelihood and a way of life, not a business for profit" (Redfield, 1956, p. 27). The peasant, in this context, is differentiated from the primitive tribesman, the "rural proletariat" (in Mintz' sense of the term), and the modern farmer with his capital and technology. This distinction is apparent in such features of peasant society as its relationship to urban markets and the almost total absence of modern machinery and tools. With respect to the world-wide and timeless characteristics of the peasant life, Redfield refers us to Hesiod's description of peasants in 6th century B.C. Greece, to Sturt's description of 19th century England, and to his own work with contemporary Maya Indians in Yucatan. His comparison of life among these three groups, so widely dispersed in time and space, showed a cluster of "three closely related attitudes and values: an intimate and reverent attitude toward the land; the idea that agricultural work is good and commerce not so good; and an emphasis on productive industry as a prime virtue" (Redfield, 1956, p. 112).

This point of view, recognizing that there are minor differences within peasant societies, assumes that there is at the same time a world-wide type of human association independent of political and economic systems, and that the people who share this association can be termed peasants. In their recent study of social character in a Mexican village, Fromm and Maccoby started from a very similar point of view (Fromm and Maccoby, 1970, pp. 1-7), as have Foster, Wolf, Nash, Thomas and Znaniecki, and others.

A final characteristic which is of importance in this paper, is that peasant societies may be viewed as being on a continuum between primitive, isolated, self-contained communities and the complex social and cultural system we call civilization. They are, in other words, part-societies, related to the market towns and under pressure to change from technology and industrialization. With this pressure for change, the qualities of life which the peasants value are perceived as threatened. By the same token, that which gives meaning to their lives is threatened, leading them to take certain steps to cope with this threat, now conservative, now progressive, but in many ways ambiguous and halting, expressing both hope and fear.

In addition to the specific problems caused by the application of industrial technology, the peasants in societies all over the world are profoundly affected by the introduction of this new culture in which they can play only a backward role. As Erich Fromm and Michael Maccoby say in *Social Character in a Mexican Village:*

> The peasant is at a double disadvantage: he has lost his own culture and does not gain the material advantages of the more affluent city population. He is not only materially poor, but is made to feel humanly backward, 'underdeveloped'.

More specifically, they have witnessed:

> the victorious march of technological industrialism destroying the traditional values and replacing them with nothing except a vague longing for the good life represented by the city. All attempts to 'improve' the peasant by making him better adapted to city life only reinforce the process of human deprivation, without giving him more than, at best, the belief in the paradise of consumption that his grandchildren might enter some day.
> (Fromm/Maccoby, 1970, p. 237)

We have to ask now—before, literally, it is too late—for a reassessment of what we mean by progress in our own culture, especially before we decide to impose it as a standard of "development" in another. Peaceful social change means not only change of physically non-violent methods, but also change in which there is no cultural shock: no jarring spiritual or psychological clash as one culture asserts its superiority over another. Our young people are trying to establish an alternate life-style, through communes and intentional communities where perhaps they can find a sense of humanity, brotherhood and love, of cooperation instead of competition, qualities which I have found again and again in the small pueblos of Mexico and South America. It seems so obvious that to say it should not be necessary; but as a nation we seem unable to realize that our culture has destroyed many simple, beautiful things which more and more people feel are necessary to live a full, humane life. Instead of destroying through ignorance these same qualities in other cultures, we should be doing everything in our power to preserve them and to learn from them. Let me assure you that I do not advocate preserving the ignorant peasant, picturesque in his native hut. But over half the world's population live in peasant villages; we must try to understand these people before we find ourselves committing cultural genocide.

Levi Strauss reinforces this position in a recent paper, commenting,

> And we should learn that *progress* sometimes consists in looking backward toward those doomed to be called primitive people we anthropologists are studying before it is too late, and who, for centuries and centuries

have placed their wisdom in protecting and keeping safe a sound equilibrium between man and environment.

(Levi-Strauss, 1972, p. 2)

For the past half century or more, anthropologists, economists, sociologists, psychologists, and others have been examining peasant societies in an effort to arrive at satisfactory theories of development, progress, and modernization. However, all too rarely have their studies taken into account the roles of women in these processes. In most of the studies cited above the word "peasant," even though itself of neutral gender, usually implies a male. (Eric Wolf's *Sons of the Shaking Earth* (1959) is one example of this, but one can find male virtues and manly attributes assumed—or even explicitly stated—as primary features of peasant societies.) Women peasants appear in the literature as sex partners of the men, as mothers of the children or as helpers, rarely if ever as individuals with hopes, abilities and functions of their own in the society. As Beverly Chiñas said:

> Up to now, one might accurately state, I think, that ethnology has been rather completely male-oriented and male dominated, making the cross-cultural investigation of women's roles and how these may interrelate with, effect, influence, and be influenced by the total system, difficult.

(Chiñas, 1971, p. 22)

In a time of unprecedented change throughout the world, peasant societies are increasingly impinged upon by the "necessities" of progress. It is crucial to learn about the roles women have to estimate their potential roles in the changes throughout the world. But, in considering women's potential role in any society, we must first understand what her current or actual role is. It is with this that we may encounter problems. As Elise Boulding says in a recent unpublished paper, "The social invisibility of women makes it difficult to document their roles in any society, in whatever stage of industrialization."

Where and how might one find new evidence about the relationships of the roles of women to change, either as they effected change or were affected by it? This study will focus on a single group of peasant women who are living in a society which has been undergoing change and which faces still more drastic modernization. It will undertake a direct investigation of the nature of women's roles as they are perceived by themselves, by others in their community, and by the writer, a trained woman observer who herself becomes part of the process she is studying by assuming the role of "activist observer".

I decided that the ideal community would be one which had been thoroughly studied by competent scholars over a relatively long period of time, for which present data could be effectively integrated into preceding data so that the nature and extent of change could be noted, and the role of women in the whole process examined in historical perspective. Chan Kom is a village that meets these criteria.

I wanted very much to find out if the beauty, the enjoyment and the dignity I had felt in my years of working with Mexican peasant women, was due to mere sentimentality on my part. Were my eyes really as blinded as Oscar Lewis and some of my friends once felt? Was I really only idealizing the "noble savage"? Or was there something nearer the truth than the "culture of poverty" which Lewis has so extensively described? Were most of the women morose, timid and male-dominated as he had projected them? Was a traditional society more "life centered" than a *mestizo* community? Were the women there more satisfied with their lives? Was work more "spiritually satisfying" than in the mestizo village where Erich Fromm and Michael Maccoby found that "work is seen by all but the most productive individuals as a necessary evil and as a means for gain" (1970, p. 20). In their study of *Social Character in a Mexican Village,* they have suggested:

> Both in medieval society and among the Mayan peasants described by Redfield, work is meant to be spiritually satisfying . . . the art, folklore and handicrafts of both the Mayan and the medieval peasant suggest a higher level of productiveness and a greater enjoyment of life than in the village we have studied.
>
> (Fromm/Maccoby, 1970, p. 120)

In my decade of field work I had spent much time visiting isolated villages of all kinds and working closely with the community leaders, men and women. However, I had always been an outsider, a community development expert, a change agent, working nearly always within an operational framework. Would I see things differently if I lived in a traditional subsistence agricultural village? If possible, I wanted to find this out as it was felt by the people who were living it, and not by those of us who were observing it.

Methods of Operation

My first intention was to study the women leaders in Chan Kom to whom others ascribed greater knowledge and to whom they looked for formal and informal advice, influence, and initiative in making decisions and taking action affecting some aspects of the life of the community. However, I found that no women were publicly defined as such, at least as far as could be ascertained so early in my dealings within the village. I decided instead to concentrate on the women of one of the leading families in Chan Kom. I did not want to use a large questionnaire, or do a macrostudy. I wanted to have the women share their life-stories with me.

Don Trinidad, the elderly village leader with whom I had worked closely in setting up my research on the roles of women, felt that it was very important to have someone in the village who really wanted to understand the women, someone with whom they could talk and discuss things the way the men did with each other and with the *ladinos* (outsiders). On my first visit he had said that he wasn't sure whether the women would talk with me, and he did not think that many of them could speak Spanish. At first the Mexican anthropologists with whom I was working suggested that I use a Mayan speaking field assistant, since the village women barely spoke Spanish. (We later agreed that the possibility of establishing a good rapport with the women would be decreased by the presence of an interpreter.) I found that the women spoke Spanish fairly well as a second language, yet that they always spoke Mayan when men were around.

During my early talks with these women I asked each if she would like to have a taped interview answering some questions I was interested in. All of them agreed. For these first interviews I used a combination of the different questionnaires mentioned earlier. Basically, I selected parts of the revised Fromm-Maccoby questionnaire, adding specific questions which would give me information on individuation covering the nine variables Boulding used: age of marriage, freedom of marriage choice, property rights, inheritance rights, divorce rights, range of movement from hearth, handler of money and/or food provider, freedom to be traders and/or business women, and tribal positions of authority.

I was especially interested in knowing how they felt about themselves, how much individuation or individualism in the Reisman and Fromm sense they had or felt that they had. I wanted to learn their capacity to discover and realize themselves as they lived and were. Mindful of Fromm's statement that his type of "freedom and individualism is bound up with economic and social changes that will permit the individual to become free in terms of realization of self" (Fromm, 1946, p. 234), I wondered how much the people of Chan Kom might lose or gain with the opening of the new roads.

The basic economic material from the Mexican National Institute of Anthropology and History fact sheet on traditionalism and modernization, with its detailed information regarding such things as size of property, and amount of earnings, caused some resistance and confusion on the part of the women. Primarily, it put too much emphasis on materialistic things and gave me in return questions from them on how much *my* shoes, my pen, or my dress cost. Gradually we were able to get into more general conversations about love and hopes and dreams. When I listen to the early tapes I am surprised at how non-committal and incomplete their first answers were. In fact I have not used these interviews as a basic part of the data following, but did incorporate them with the later material which the women spontaneously shared with me. The questionnaires served a real purpose, however, in that they projected several areas of interest; gradually the women chose different subjects in which they became kinds of specialists, as will be seen in the vignettes which follow for key women. I feel that the original interviews were less threatening than our later, more open conversations, and these later talks may not have been possible without the more structured encounters from which we started. The formality of the situation lent importance to the information the women were sharing, and to them, as the key figures in this new study of Chan Kom. The questionnaires, the taped interviews, all the *papeleria* really made them feel good—and yet, because this was the first time anyone outside had ever asked them about how they felt about things, they were also a little overwhelmed and shy.

As for recounting the stories of their lives, this seemed a new experience. "I was born—I played with my brothers and sisters—my mother, my grandmother taught me to make tortillas . . . I got married. . . ." I found that sex and related matters of womanhood are not discussed openly. The women explained to me that it was considered a sin to tell a girl about menstruation before her first period, or to explain sex to her before marriage. They had not instructed their daughters, nor had their mothers instructed them. They did not seem to discuss these things among themselves; during my first visit they seemed shy, perhaps embarrassed by my questions relating to these topics, and sometimes pretended not to understand my Spanish. On my second visit, however, they had grown to trust me and were eager to talk. It seemed that all of the pent-up emotions and questions came pouring out of them. They felt I was someone with whom they could talk about their concerns. I could hardly stop them to ask questions of my own.

I came into Chan Kom as a foreigner, and wanted to avoid imposing views from an alien culture, however, I soon found that I could not remain a completely passive observer. It seemed extremely important to understand and to be sensitive to the local situation in order to work there in a culturally non-polluting, human way. I agree very much with

Freire, who believes that "to impose one ideology or prove a theory is another form of cultural oppression" and that "creative dialogue between researcher and object-subject turns into a process of mutual learning." (1971) Partly because of these convictions, and partly because I found that I learned most when the women led the conversation, I put aside my original research design, including the carefully translated questionnaires, the schedules, the collection of data for comparison and statistical analysis. I decided instead to gather the substance of my study from "creative dialogues."

I made repeated field trips of varying lengths to Chan Kom between March, 1971 and July, 1972, and have continued my contact with the village since that time. I have talked at length with the wife, daughters, and daughters-in-law of Don Trinidad, one of the leaders of the community. It was through these women and their networks of friends that I have been able to get some feeling for the life of the Mayan woman. The women range in age from seventeen to sixty-five. In fact, with children and grandchildren, grandmothers and aunts, cousins and friends, I reached many other age groups.

Later let me introduce briefly each of these women whom I came to know so well, and tell you how I got to know them and their friends, as I tried to understand their roles in daily life as they faced imminent change. But first, let me tell how I got in to Chan Kom.

Three Dimensions

Establishing a Human Network

When I decided to visit Chan Kom to see if it seemed a suitable place to do my field work, I had great difficulty in getting there. Even though I knew from the literature that it was only twelve kilometers from Chichen Itza, there was a great vagueness in the information about how to go. I had spent the night in the guest house of the Protestant clinic in Xochenpich; people there had not been very helpful in telling me how I should go. "There is no bus. . .you'll have to walk. . .It's two leagues. . . ." I decided to check in Pisté at the general store, which had the only phone in town. Maybe they could help. The first reply I received was "Why go to Chan Kom? Stay away. It may even be dangerous." The family running the store turned out to be one of the former leading families of Chan Kom. They were part of the Protestant

Freire, who believes that "to impose one ideology or prove a theory is another form of cultural oppression" and that "creative dialogue between researcher and object-subject turns into a process of mutual learning." (1971) Partly because of these convictions, and partly because I found that I learned most when the women led the conversation, I put aside my original research design, including the carefully translated questionnaires, the schedules, the collection of data for comparison and statistical analysis. I decided instead to gather the substance of my study from "creative dialogues."

I made repeated field trips of varying lengths to Chan Kom between March, 1971 and July, 1972, and have continued my contact with the village since that time. I have talked at length with the wife, daughters, and daughters-in-law of Don Trinidad, one of the leaders of the community. It was through these women and their networks of friends that I have been able to get some feeling for the life of the Mayan woman. The women range in age from seventeen to sixty-five. In fact, with children and grandchildren, grandmothers and aunts, cousins and friends, I reached many other age groups.

Later let me introduce briefly each of these women whom I came to know so well, and tell you how I got to know them and their friends, as I tried to understand their roles in daily life as they faced imminent change. But first, let me tell how I got in to Chan Kom.

Three Dimensions

Establishing a Human Network

When I decided to visit Chan Kom to see if it seemed a suitable place to do my field work, I had great difficulty in getting there. Even though I knew from the literature that it was only twelve kilometers from Chichen Itza, there was a great vagueness in the information about how to go. I had spent the night in the guest house of the Protestant clinic in Xochenpich; people there had not been very helpful in telling me how I should go. "There is no bus. . .you'll have to walk. . .It's two leagues. . . ." I decided to check in Pisté at the general store, which had the only phone in town. Maybe they could help. The first reply I received was "Why go to Chan Kom? Stay away. It may even be dangerous." The family running the store turned out to be one of the former leading families of Chan Kom. They were part of the Protestant

preceding data so that the nature and extent of change could be noted, and the role of women in the whole process examined in historical perspective. Chan Kom is a village that meets these criteria.

I wanted very much to find out if the beauty, the enjoyment and the dignity I had felt in my years of working with Mexican peasant women, was due to mere sentimentality on my part. Were my eyes really as blinded as Oscar Lewis and some of my friends once felt? Was I really only idealizing the "noble savage"? Or was there something nearer the truth than the "culture of poverty" which Lewis has so extensively described? Were most of the women morose, timid and male-dominated as he had projected them? Was a traditional society more "life centered" than a *mestizo* community? Were the women there more satisfied with their lives? Was work more "spiritually satisfying" than in the mestizo village where Erich Fromm and Michael Maccoby found that "work is seen by all but the most productive individuals as a necessary evil and as a means for gain" (1970, p. 20). In their study of *Social Character in a Mexican Village,* they have suggested:

> Both in medieval society and among the Mayan peasants described by Redfield, work is meant to be spiritually satisfying . . . the art, folklore and handicrafts of both the Mayan and the medieval peasant suggest a higher level of productiveness and a greater enjoyment of life than in the village we have studied.

(Fromm/Maccoby, 1970, p. 120)

In my decade of field work I had spent much time visiting isolated villages of all kinds and working closely with the community leaders, men and women. However, I had always been an outsider, a community development expert, a change agent, working nearly always within an operational framework. Would I see things differently if I lived in a traditional subsistence agricultural village? If possible, I wanted to find this out as it was felt by the people who were living it, and not by those of us who were observing it.

Methods of Operation

My first intention was to study the women leaders in Chan Kom to whom others ascribed greater knowledge and to whom they looked for formal and informal advice, influence, and initiative in making decisions and taking action affecting some aspects of the life of the community. However, I found that no women were publicly defined as such, at least as far as could be ascertained so early in my dealings within the village. I decided instead to concentrate on the women of

one of the leading families in Chan Kom. I did not want to use a large
questionnaire, or do a macrostudy. I wanted to have the women share
their life-stories with me.

Don Trinidad, the elderly village leader with whom I had worked
closely in setting up my research on the roles of women, felt that it was
very important to have someone in the village who really wanted to
understand the women, someone with whom they could talk and discuss things the way the men did with each other and with the *ladinos*
(outsiders). On my first visit he had said that he wasn't sure whether
the women would talk with me, and he did not think that many of them
could speak Spanish. At first the Mexican anthropologists with whom
I was working suggested that I use a Mayan speaking field assistant,
since the village women barely spoke Spanish. (We later agreed that
the possibility of establishing a good rapport with the women would
be decreased by the presence of an interpreter.) I found that the
women spoke Spanish fairly well as a second language, yet that they
always spoke Mayan when men were around.

During my early talks with these women I asked each if she would
like to have a taped interview answering some questions I was interested in. All of them agreed. For these first interviews I used a combination of the different questionnaires mentioned earlier. Basically, I
selected parts of the revised Fromm-Maccoby questionnaire, adding
specific questions which would give me information on individuation
covering the nine variables Boulding used: age of marriage, freedom
of marriage choice, property rights, inheritance rights, divorce rights,
range of movement from hearth, handler of money and/or food provider, freedom to be traders and/or business women, and tribal positions of authority.

I was especially interested in knowing how they felt about themselves, how much individuation or individualism in the Reisman and
Fromm sense they had or felt that they had. I wanted to learn their
capacity to discover and realize themselves as they lived and were.
Mindful of Fromm's statement that his type of "freedom and individualism is bound up with economic and social changes that will permit
the individual to become free in terms of realization of self" (Fromm,
1946, p. 234), I wondered how much the people of Chan Kom might
lose or gain with the opening of the new roads.

The basic economic material from the Mexican National Institute of
Anthropology and History fact sheet on traditionalism and modernization, with its detailed information regarding such things as size of
property, and amount of earnings, caused some resistance and confu-

sion on the part of the women. Primarily, it put too much
materialistic things and gave me in return questions from
much *my* shoes, my pen, or my dress cost. Gradually we
get into more general conversations about love and hopes
When I listen to the early tapes I am surprised at how nor
and incomplete their first answers were. In fact I have not
interviews as a basic part of the data following, but did ir
them with the later material which the women spontaneou
with me. The questionnaires served a real purpose, howeve
they projected several areas of interest; gradually the wom
different subjects in which they became kinds of specialists,
seen in the vignettes which follow for key women. I feel
original interviews were less threatening than our later, mo
conversations, and these later talks may not have been possib
out the more structured encounters from which we started. T
mality of the situation lent importance to the information the
were sharing, and to them, as the key figures in this new study o
Kom. The questionnaires, the taped interviews, all the *papeleria*
made them feel good—and yet, because this was the first time a
outside had ever asked them about how they felt about things,
were also a little overwhelmed and shy.

As for recounting the stories of their lives, this seemed a new ex
ence. "I was born—I played with my brothers and sisters—my mot
my grandmother taught me to make tortillas . . . I got married. .
I found that sex and related matters of womanhood are not discuss
openly. The women explained to me that it was considered a sin to t
a girl about menstruation before her first period, or to explain sex
her before marriage. They had not instructed their daughters, nor ha
their mothers instructed them. They did not seem to discuss thes
things among themselves; during my first visit they seemed shy, per
haps embarrassed by my questions relating to these topics, and sometimes pretended not to understand my Spanish. On my second visit,
however, they had grown to trust me and were eager to talk. It seemed
that all of the pent-up emotions and questions came pouring out of
them. They felt I was someone with whom they could talk about their
concerns. I could hardly stop them to ask questions of my own.

I came into Chan Kom as a foreigner, and wanted to avoid imposing
views from an alien culture, however, I soon found that I could not
remain a completely passive observer. It seemed extremely important
to understand and to be sensitive to the local situation in order to work
there in a culturally non-polluting, human way. I agree very much with

group run out by the Catholics in 1955 when the two groups shot it
out in the town square. It had been cousin against cousin, neighbor
against neighbor, brother against sister. The Catholics had won, and
almost all the Protestants had left Chan Kom. When they found out
that I was really serious agout going, and not just asking questions,
they looked at the map in my copy of *The Village That Chose Progress*
and showed me where the road turned off to the right into the underbrush just after Chichen Itza and the caves of Balanchine.

> Take a right hand road. You can tell where it is by the red mud on the
> highway. But it's really impassable. Sometimes heavy trucks get through
> but often they get stuck. You can walk it in about three hours. . .but it's
> muddy on the road and you can't get through the underbrush.

Could I rent a jeep? No. Could a VW go through? No. Finally I
arranged with a farmer in Xochenpich to take me in on Sunday, his day
off, in the old jeep that belonged to the Clinic (and was fortunately not
marked as such). He and I stopped again in Pisté and talked with the
Puucs before starting on to Chan Kom. Some older women, wives of
the two brothers, were there this time, and they scanned the photos
in the book intently.

> Look! There's Luz. She saved Gerónimo's life when he was just three. The
> *yerbatero* and the *h-men* had come—we had done everything but Geróni-
> mo was dying. Then Doña Luz came and gave him some medicine. She
> saved his life. Tell her, Señora, that we remember. . .

We tore ourselves away from the excited women and started for
Chan Kom; we wanted to get in and out before the afternoon rains.
I had with me my canvas briefcase, with *The Village That Chose
Progress,* my journal, a tape recorder, a sweater and jeans, and some
cheese, bread, tomato juice and fruit for a picnic lunch. The driver had
his five year old son and a loaded gun. Why? "To shoot deer or birds,"
he assured me. But with the repeated stories of violence, recorded and
verbal, I would have preferred to have gone unarmed in a "Protestant"
jeep.

We found the turn-off. The road was in terrible shape, great boul-
ders and deep mudholes, but above and around us the jungle was
beautiful. There were lots of strange birds and great quietness—just
water dripping from the leaves and bird calls. I felt a tenseness on the
part of the driver. The jeep was old, and he kept saying he wasn't sure
it would make it. After two and a half hours we reached an elevated
road, narrow but smooth, turned left, and in a few minutes we were
on the plaza of Chan Kom. We turned right and parked just in front
of a large boulder in front of a house. Don Trini walked out; I had

arrived and was being greeted. On informing him that I had come to see the "village that chose progress," I was asked whether I knew Redfield and Villa Rojas. Upon answering that I admired them both very much and had worked with Villa Rojas in Chiapas, every door was opened to me. "Professor Villa is our friend—our *compadre*. No one has had so much influence on our village as he. He was here in February. He's going to help me finish my autobiography—he's already put some of my history on his tape recorder," Don Trini told me. As I explained my hope to do a study of women in a Mexican village, I was urged to stay, to do my study there. "Why don't you stay now? The highway truck is coming Tuesday and you can go out with it. You can have Professor Villa's room." The planning of the trip had been difficult, and the driver was obviously ready to leave. I accepted their invitation, but took the precaution of telling the driver, "If I haven't come back to Xochenpich by Tuesday will you come back for me?" The farmer promised; I gave him half the picnic, and he and his son started back.

Don Trini and his son, Antonio, took me on a visit to the school, the pride of the village.

> Professor Villa was our teacher here for four years. He taught our children and us about many things. It was because of him that Redfield came, and the Carnegie group. Professor Villa is still our friend, he still comes. He was here in February. We hope he decides to live here—maybe he will when the new road comes.

Then Don Trini took me back to where we had parked the car earlier, through a bare dark room into a rocky yard where a thatched hut stood between several stone walls. "There is Doña Luz, who will take care of you. She took care of the Redfields, so she knows how to keep Americans in good health. Don't worry." And looking at Doña Luz I knew I need not worry. I knew too that she was a woman I would like to know well. Very quickly she brought me a hammock, a chamber pot, and a chair and table; the room I had walked through became my room for three days, but it also continued to be the entrance to the thatched hut in the yard and the exit to the plaza for the numerous pigs who seemed to resent my closing the door. In fact, I couldn't really shut the back door, because it didn't have any hinges but was just a heavy two-fold screen that covered most of the opening. The door opening on the plaza was hinged on both sides and seemed adequately closed with a stone in front, but when night came I became aware of the many eyes peering in through the cracks.

Don Trini suggested that I rest a while. I asked whether he had a book on Chan Kom, since I had arrived with only Redfield's last study, *A Village That Chose Progress*. Much to my surprise and pleasure he appeared in a few minutes with the original English Carnegie report, complete and unabridged. It was in tattered condition, with pages out of order, but carefully stamped, "Property of the Village of Chan Kom." This book was a great help to me during the next few days, as I oriented myself to the village, asked for explanations of the pictures, and in turn translated parts the people were interested in. Looking through the report I caught my breath as I realized I had not only arrived but was in; was in fact stranded without any of the field precautions—no aspirin, no halizone, not even a change of clothes. At the same time it seemed right.

Doña Luz came to the door and asked whether I was hungry. I was starving and went into the hut with her. We talked about the Redfields, about the Villa Rojas', and about my interest in talking with the women of Chan Kom. Luz knew about Don Trini's autobiography, and seemed pleased that I wanted to talk with her about her self and not just to be fed. She gave me water, a fresh towel to dry my hands, and showed me a chair at the scrubbed table, one end of which was covered with a clean white cloth embroidered with birds and flowers. We chatted as she made thin round tortillas on a low mahogany stool by the hearth fire. She made them in a way I had never seen before: instead of patting them between her two hands as I had watched for thirty years in villages in many parts of Mexico, she turned the *masa* rapidly on the table top and patted it deftly with her fingers. And there was a beautifully thin, round tortilla ready for the *comal*.

I gave her the message from the Puucs about their remembering her saving Gerónimo's life. From that moment on I felt that in Luz I had a special friend. Not only was she my hostess but my guide to the past, particularly in regard to Mayan ritual: the *loh casa* (ceremonial cleansing of a new thatched hut) on my first night there, and on later visits, the handwashing ceremony and the *Pib*. She is the *curandera* ("curer") for Chan Kom and neighboring *rancherias*. If I got up early enough in the morning I could watch her having office hours in the kitchen, giving different kinds of herbal medicines. Doña Luz is a key figure in Chan Kom, and not just because of her status as Don Trini's wife.

As we talked we were joined in the kitchen by a lovely looking young woman. "This is Ana, the wife of my son Jorge. They eat with us but their house is on the corner where the *nixtamal* is." Ana is twenty-four, and runs one of the four *molinos* (gasoline-operated grist mills) in town, an important position. She has more time for this than most women because she has only one child. Ana is intelligent about business matters, selling fruits, vegetables, sewing, and the rights to her well, She is naturally beautiful, quiet and very domestic, vain, and independent. As she moved through stages of curing her illness, from *h-men,* to the herbalist, and finally to the doctor in town, she seemed a transitional figure. It was she who shared her dreams so freely with me, and who, by dreaming of me, followed my direction to the clinic to see the doctor.

As I watched Ana and Luz making more tortillas and ate my beans and eggs, a very different looking woman came in—taller, heavier, and dressed in modern clothes. This was Flora, the wife of Antonio, whom I had just met, and the mother of all the other children who seemed to flow in and out of the hut. She sat down with a handsome nursing baby at her breast and a knee baby leaning against her and joined the other two making tortillas. Flora was an integral part of my life in Chan Kom, but I was never able to reach the same rapport with her that I did with most of the others. She, her husband, and their six children (three of whom are loaned to relatives) are strangely interwoven in the family network. They will, I predict, be the earliest marginal family, lost somewhere between tradition and urbanization.

While we talked, first Antonio joined me at the table, then Jorge, and finally Don Trini. There seemed to be no specific time or order for their meal that I could observe, but the making of tortillas went on for several hours during which all of the extended family were fed, with the women eating last around the hearth where they had fed the children.

Just before sunset the children and adults started appearing, all scrubbed looking. Seeing Ana come back fresh, obviously from a bath, I suddenly felt tired and dusty and asked if I might have a bath too. Doña Luz ceremoniously took me across the plaza to the house of Gabriela, Don Trini's daughter. She said that this house was a "bathroom . . . which would be better for you." Gabriela was most welcoming, but evidently the bathroom was being used as a store room. Quickly it was cleaned of bottles and rubbish and the fence of straw placed across the patio adjoining it was moved so that I could enter. One of the children swept the floor, and I was given a bar of soap, a pail of warm water, and an old, clean cloth to dry with. I was also given a small stool—to sit on, I supposed. I was delighted to be able to get off the dirt which had accumulated from the jeep ride as well as the walks in the dusty plaza. A passage from Hernandez, a 19th century Mayologist, came to mind:

> . . . once they have reached eleven or twelve years of age, (Mayan women) always appear as clean as possible, taking pains to wash themselves and comb their hair with as much fastidiousness as if they were about to take a stroll.
>
> (Hernandez, 1943, p. 272)

After my bath we chatted a few minutes, and Gabriela soon became another key person in my understanding of Chan Kom. The only widow in the village that I got to know well, she works her own *milpa* "like a man." as the others say.

In the afternoon I was taken on a tour of the plaza to see the town hall, complete with arches on its portals. I noticed strange holes which Don Trini explained were for guns, so soldiers could hide and protect the town; we did not pursue this at the time. Instead we went to the corner store, run by his son Eduardo with a great deal of help from his seventeen year old daughter, Felicia. There I bought toothpaste and a candle and met another family who became an intergral part of my daily living. Amparo, Eduardo's wife, bakes bread professionally with the help of her daughters. This is an extremely close knit family; they think of themselves as a cooperative. The family is very literate, in contrast to the others in the village, and Amparo wants each of her daughters to have a profession. In fact, they may go to live with their aunt in Mérida in order to learn. Amparo is extremely religious—she has a beautiful home shrine to Fátima and is close to the priest. As a mother of eight Amparo is always busy, but never frantic; warm and adaptable, she is a strong personality.

Before escorting me back to my room, Don Trini took me to meet another son, Alvaro, who is mayor of Chan Kom for a third term. He is married to Victoria, who I later found out was a sister of both Amparo and Flora. She is a hearty, vigorous person who loves sewing and work. Victoria is quicktempered and bossy, but with a good sense of humor and enormous curiosity. She considers herself an artist because of the intricate designs she weaves into her *huipiles,* and indeed she does beautiful work. Victoria and Alvaro have no living children of their own, but two sons of Flora's are living with them. On my second visit to Chan Kom, Victoria invited me to live in her upstairs room, because she had accepted me as a fellow artist when she saw me sketching the house on the square. This was a perfect solution to a problem I had not known how to solve. The noise of the pigs and the complete lack of privacy from the plaza and yard were becoming more and more difficult, so I accepted her invitation with a sigh of relief. From this vantage point I could sketch the plaza, draw the plan of the village, and also have peace and quiet.

From then on during my field trips to Chan Kom I lived as a member of an extended family—sleeping in my hammock in a vacant room at Victoria's—eating in Luz's community kitchen with Flora and her children—doing my laundry in a hollow log near Ana's well—having my daily bath, which is practically a ceremony there, at Gabriela's—and buying the few things I needed such as candles, soap, and alcohol for my little stove to boil my water from Felicia and freshly baked bread from Amparo, her mother. I found a natural living network where I moved without plan from one part of the day to another, without appointments, without timing, but still feeling that I had not disturbed the lovely rhythm which I felt was such a real part of their lives. When they saw me coming they would know for what need I was coming.

I felt that the rising and the setting of the sun controlled the patterns of life, and within a short time I had readjusted my daily life to theirs. I was awake to see the sunrise and asleep in my hammock soon after the turkeys became quiet, each in his special place on the stone wall. The swallows had dived into the *cenote* and the fireflies were coming out; I could watch the stars, so incredibly bright above the dark plaza, only a blinking candle or two in the houses around the square. Gradually my acquaintances grew, and by the locations of candles I knew who was awake around the plaza.

My network now included a key family on each of the four sides of the village square, and I joined the parade of people crossing and recrossing this commons. Soon I had met the other children of Don Trini and their households. First was Anita, the second wife of Demetrio, Don Trini's oldest son. My first impression of Anita was a negative one: She seemed quite aggressive and I thought that her children appeared poorly cared for in comparison with the others. After many hours of talking with her, however, I came to feel that she was one of the brightest, most sensitive of the women. She has a real ability to encourage creative learning among her children. But Anita is not really accepted in Chan Kom. She is viewed as a second wife, an outsider with no relatives in the village.

And then there was Marta who was living in a grass hut on a side street, another daughter of Don Trini. I was pleased at first to be meeting families away from the main square, but at the end of our first conversation, Marta told me they had just arranged to buy one of the houses on the plaza. With this move all of Don Trini's children in Chan Kom will be living on the main square, owning all the corner properties except one. I came to know the people in the other houses, I finally realized that including the family of Don Trini's uncle-stepfather, Don

Pascual (three of whose children have married Don Trini's children), all of the private dwellings on the square except one belonged to the Mecab family. Redfield had commented both in 1934 and 1948 on the existence of three "great" families who had originally staked out certain sides of the plaza when the village was organized. Now we have only one leading family who live and work in much the same way as do their relatives and neighbors scattered throughout this community. With progress brought by the new highway and increased commercialization, economic differences and perhaps ever more stratification will probably result.

But back to Marta, who is much lighter-skinned than the other children of Don Trini, and said to resemble her dead mother, Doña Hilaria. She is fat, happy, with an earthy, almost raucous laugh. Marta's husband, Rufino, makes *milpa,* that is, raises corn in the ancient slash-burn method, still using a planting stick—no plow, no hoe, no commercial fertilizer. She and the children often help him in the fields. Their front room was piled high with corn when I stopped by in November, and I was shown the fullness of the ears, the beauty of the grain. It was like a flower arrangement. "It was a good year," said Rufino. They are very close, though not closed to others—gregarious people.

We wouldn't have the family picture complete without Beatriz, the oldest daughter of Don Trini. She had married one of the young Mayans working with Morley on the original excavation at Chichen Itza. When I called on her in her modern home in Mérida, the capital of Yucatan, after making an appointment by telephone, I was very curious. How had she changed? Had she rejected the past after leaving Chan Kom? Even though she was in city clothes I could see a strong family resemblance; as we talked, there was great warmth in her voice as she spoke of her family and her old home.

> I married when I was just seventeen. My father arranged everything, but I have been very happy. My daughters married much later than I did though, one at twenty-one and one at twenty-five. And they chose their own husbands. . . . I am happy here, but I still like to go back to Chan Kom. Miguel and I have just bought the house on the plaza beside my father's home. . . . Aren't you going to stay for the Fiesta? My children's *nana,* Demetrio's daughter by his first wife, has already gone. And Felicia spent last night here. I wish that Amparo and Eduardo would let her come study in Mérida. She could live here with me. Felicia is so bright. . . . I love to have the nieces and nephews come to my home.

We talked for a long time, and I came to the conclusion that, as I had been told in the village, this was truly a half way station between the village and city.

Although not a close member of the extended family group on which
I was concentrating, Berta was drawn to my attention because she is
the first and only female member of the town council. Later I learned
her father was Don Trini's half-brother who had Castillianized his
name. Her husband Juan, the town clerk, spoke proudly of her to me
and invited me to their home to interview her. During my visit I was
immediately struck by how different their home was in comparison to
the others in Chan Kom. It seemed to belong to another part of
Mexico—mestizo Mexican and not Mayan. Berta and her family wore
modern clothes as well, dresses rather than *huipiles,* factory made
trousers, plastic shoes. Why such a difference? In our conversations I
learned that Berta's father had been a member of the first Rural Cultural Mission to come to Chan Kom, and that many of her ideas and
attitudes, particularly concerning education, were greatly influenced
by him. She was proud that theirs was the only family in Chan Kom
who sent children away to a good school in Mérida. We spoke also of
her unique position on the council. She is the council secretary, and
keeps all the records on the various meetings. In addition, she helps
her husband with his job as *registro civil,* and is capable of taking over
for him when he leaves town. "I have a key to the office," she told me,
smiling.

Another woman who was outside the extended family I was focusing
on impressed me greatly as a key figure in Chan Kom. She is Concepción, the midwife who is married to Ramón, the bonesetter of the
village. She is also sister of the local *h-men* (shaman and priest) and
their father was a shaman also. At Luz's invitation, I had attended the
pib, the hand washing and other Mayan ceremonies at Concepción's
house. As she spoke only Mayan, my interview with her was conducted
through her eldest son. I originally asked that a daughter translate for
us, but Concepción smiled and said that her son would do. "He knows
of these things. He helped his wife when their two children were born,
as most Mayan fathers do" she added. In our discussion, I learned that
she also worked as a housekeeper for the priest when he visited Chan
Kom, and I wondered at such an odd combination. Had he chosen her
as a link with the pagan way of life that still influences Chan Kom, or
had she chosen him? Concepción told me that no one had taught her
to be a midwife, not even as a child. She simply had dreams that told
her how to do the various things, dreams about each woman she took
care of. "No one had ever died under my care," she told me. We spoke
of the massages and different treatments for pregnant women, their
diets, the rules they should follow. She said that she charged the same

amount to deliver girls and boys, but the women all told me they were charged more for the boys. Why? "Because they will bring more money to the family when they are grown." Concepción is, to me, a beautiful dignified woman with a completely professional attitude toward her job. She and Doña Luz seem to me to be the most respected women in Chan Kom. Their power and influence are not obvious, but they form a pervasive undercurrent in the life of the village. These two relate most closely to the Mayan past, with their knowledge of medicine, of herbs, and secrets.

I should point out here that Chan Kom is not a typical Mayan village and these women were not necessarily typical of Chan Kom. Even though most of the women who were more deeply involved in this study were related to the leading family, and as such held positions where they potentially could claim more "status through wealth" than others when modernization gives it more importance, I felt a great similarity between them and the other women of the community. They wore the same clothing, ate the same food, drew water from the same wells, had children in the same school, and enjoyed the same communal rights. Every family has a home lot and a right to *ejido* land, so there are no peons. Everybody is a peasant! Even though all of the women I have mentioned have masonry houses, most of their daily life—and the nights for many, including the family patriarch and his wife—takes place in *jacales* (thatched huts) built behind the masonry ones. Alfonso Villa Rójas notes that, "As wives of leaders, as members of the leading family, these women are setting the trend." They are at the pressure-point of change.

Regional Setting

All of us know something about the Mayan Indians, their calendar, their astronomy, their amazing ruined "cities." No single aboriginal group in the Americas has been of so much interest to international scholars for a century and a half. Some have said the Mayans were to the Aztecs what the Greeks were to the Romans. (Thompson, 1954, p. 268) Not many of us realize that the Maya, over 2 million in number, are still the largest single block of American Indians north of Peru. At the same time the Maya have maintained their cultural identity and are concentrated in Mexico, Guatemala and British Honduras (Vogt, 1969, p. 7, 21-28)

All of the contempory Mayan-speaking Indians probably differentiated, linguistically and culturally, from a small proto-Maya community of about 5,000 people in northwestern Guatemala where they cultivated maize around 2600 B.C. These later dispersed to form the present-day Maya, who are divided into two groups, the lowland and the highland Indians. The latter are divided into two groups, those in Chiapas and those in Guatemala. The lowland Mayans are divided into three groups. There are approximately three hundred people still living in a hunting and fishing group of nearly extinct Lacandon Indians in the lowland of Chiapas next to the Guatemalan border. The second group, the Huastecs, with about 60,000 people, live in Vera Cruz and are more separated from the other Mayan Indians. The largest single group of any of these Mayans are the Yucatec, who live in Champeche, Quintana Roo, and Yucatan. According to the 1970 census they number approximately 500,000. Our interest is in the lowland Mayans of Yucatan-Itza: the Yucatec women in three small rural communities near the ancient ceremonial capital of Chichen, Xochempich, Pisté, and most important of all, Chan Kom.

Many people asked me why I had gone to Chan Kom. Had it not been over-studied? What was there of interest now? As I have said, my primary concern was to select a village that had been studied in depth over a period of time, one in which I could contribute material on the role of women as the women see themselves, as they feel they have participated in their village. I wanted to gather, in their own words, how they see their daily lives, relationships to their homes, children, husbands, community, and world. I wanted to know their hopes, ambitions, fears—whatever they wished to share with me. I wanted to find out also whether life in one traditional peasant society had to be impoverished by progress. Is there any way to maintain quality of life with the "modernization of civilization"? Perhaps their society, a more traditional one, could teach ours something about progress and how best we all might face change.

A little background on the village of Chan Kom itself is necessary. In 1905 only about five *wattle* houses were built around the *cenote,* one of the natural wells in the limestone cover of Yucatan. As a ninety-nine year old informant told me, the deer used to come down to drink, and there were plum and other fruit trees around the *cenote.* The village is in the area between the *henequen* plantations and the more tropical jungle, where the Mayans over many generations have lived on subsistence corn farming. Even to this day many people are still using the slash and burn method of farming combined with the planting stick as an agricultural tool.

The land around Chan Kom, according to most references, was

settled in ancient Mayan times, but in 1847, during the War of the Castes, it was abandoned, as were many of the neighboring villages. Gradually it was resettled. Around 1920, the time of Felipe Carillo-Puerto, the socialist governor of Yucatan, this village decided that it wanted freedom from a neighboring village, its own school, and its own work projects. The people built a school at a time when there were only 100 people living around the *cenote.* They then decided to try to become the county seat. In 1923 they filed a petition for their *ejido* land, which was granted in 1926, the first settlement in their territory to gain this status: "The happiest day of my life," recalled Don Pascual, the 99 year old original settler.

Chan Kom is a free community where everyone has his own house, *solar* (or lot) and private farmlands, although there is also communal land (the *ejido)* that is shared. It is not traditional in the sense of having only descendants of its original settlers, but it is made up of Indians with shared cultural patterns. Many of the family names are the same as in the 16th century reports of the area. Most of the families have come from the nearby villages as pioneers, as people who wanted to build a new life together, or perhaps to escape the life where they were. Communal work had been very much a part of the town, and many people who left did so because they didn't want to contribute as much free labor. Redfield said that this community was made up of "ready made Calvinists" who wanted a secure future, moral gain by the fruits of their labor (Redfield, 1950, p. 158).

But this is another story—the story of how Chan Kom grew, of how the wells were drilled, how the Rural Cultural Mission came in 1945, how they built the little theatre on a rocky part of the plaza near the *cenote,* how they used the stone from the ancient Mayan oratorio to build two churches, one Protestant and one Catholic, both by voluntary labor. Perhaps we should say they were built by work contributed to the community, which was required of every man except for musicians, town officials, and sacristans. Maybe this is why there are three bands in Chan Kom! Or is it love of music?

At the same time, there is a very close relationship to the Mayan gods, the Mayan past. Chichen Itza is a short way from Chan Kom, as is one of the ancient Mayan *sacbés.* A *sacbé* is a broad, raised stone highway fifteen feet wide which cuts straight through the jungle for sixty miles from Cobá to Yaxuna, two important archeological zones of the classic, or even pre-classic period.

In a recent newspaper article Chan Kom was called a "Mayan paradise" (Sol de Yucatan, October 22, 1971). Some people would question this. They would say that in the rainy season the plaza was filled with mud and that it took two and a half hours to walk through the muddy paths to reach it. In the dry season, the plaza was a dusty field where the pigs, turkeys, and dogs gathered, and children played together.

In 1970, according to the *registro civil,* Chan Kom had 130 men over eighteen who were registered on a list as eligible to vote. There is no list for the women, but I was told that there were about the same number as men and that they also voted. (Their hands were stamped, as were the men's, to show their participation in the elections; this was also done, of course, to keep people from voting twice) The total number of inhabitants was 415, divided among 82 families, with names indicating a great deal of intermarriage. Some belonged to the families of the original settlers, and others to new families who had moved in, mostly from isolated ranches nearby.

There were seventy-three births, thirty deaths and four marriages. (Only one death was from causes other than illness. A 21 year old boy drowned in a *cenote* between Chan Kom and a neighboring village. According to the civil register this was investigated and two boys were accused of murdering him before throwing the body in the *cenote.* Apparently they had been drinking heavily at a fiesta and the violence had occurred afterward.) No divorces had been registered in thirty years, the last having been granted in 1940.

When I started my field work in Chan Kom, it was still a village of less than 450 people but had become the dreamed-of county seat, heading a *municipio* of approximately 3,000 people. It was still tiny, however, with no electricity, no running water, no plumbing, no telephone. The narrow rough path, which could not be used by automobiles, was passable only by those few heavy trucks that were willing to have their tires shredded. During the past forty years innumerable hours had been spent trying to build four different roads to reach the highway, to reach civilization, to tie Chan Kom with the modern world. Its first road had been cut straight through the jungle. The villagers had built a tower fifty feet high out of tree trunks so they could sight the tower of Chichen Itza as their mark—a link both to modern civilization and to their ancestral civilization; they had called it "the road to the light" (Redfield, 1950, p. 16). During my last visit the fourth road to be built during the last forty years, the first one that is really passable for private cars and busses, was formally opened by the Governor of Yucatan.

Mayan Framework

We are fortunate in possessing a wealth of information about the Maya, notably on the brilliant growth of Mayan civilization in the lowlands, which include the Yucatan area. But we are faced with the unsolved question of what happened to bring about the collapse of Mayan civilzation. The Spanish conquest of the Mayans extended from 1527 to 1697, with the final surrender of the Itzá in Guatemala. The conquest of Yucatan itself lasted only until 1546 with the capital of Mérida being founded in 1542, built on the site of the ancient city of Tiho.

During the 16th and 17th centuries there were a number of excellent ethnographic studies and observations on the Mayan people, by Spaniards in their early conquests, and later by Indian writers. The most comprehensive ethnological study to emerge from the Mayan zone in the 16th century was the *Relación de las Cosas de Yucatan,* which was written about 1566 by Diego de Landa. De Landa was a Franciscan who arrived in Yucatan in 1549, learned to speak Mayan, and later became Bishop of Yucatan. Among his sources were the Indian codices (which he later ordered destroyed), Indian informants, including Mayan priests, and direct observations of Mayan life. This work has been translated and edited eight times. Tozzer's eighth edition, released in 1941, is an invaluable source with its ample footnotes and bibliography.

There is a great deal of material in this early work on Mayan women, but reading it today one wonders what the women would have said about their lives, religion, and the way they felt to a Spanish bishop who was also a Franciscan, a member of the conquering race, and a man. At the same time many of the 16th century descriptions of homes, of dress, and of rituals and customs are uncannily accurate of life today.

A number of ethnological investigations have been undertaken since de Landa. In 1838 Jean Frederic Waldeck published the results of his explorations which served to stimulate the interest of John L. Stephen, who published two valuable works in 1841 and 1843. Later in the nineteenth century two Frenchmen, Augustus la Plogeon (1874) and Desiré Charnay (1882) arrived in Yucatan independently and recorded their observations, which are now available. A German geographer, Karl Sapper, covered most of the Maya area from 1888 to 1895, and published his findings in 1897. Early in the present century, Alfred M. Tozzer carried out investigations among the Maya and Lacandon (Villa Rojas, 1969, p. 240).

Then, between 1914 and 1958, the Carnegie Institute of Washington carried out its extensive research projects in Mayan archeology and ethnology under the direction first of Morley, later of Kidder, then of Pollock. The major ethnological work was done between 1930 and 1950, with some of the outstanding research being done by Steggerda, Shattuck, Thompson, and Gann, with great contributions by Robert Redfield and Alfonso Villa Rojas, as well as others in the specific area we are now discussing. Many know Chan Kom from *A Village that Chose Progress,* which Redfield wrote after returning to Chan Kom in 1948. This was seventeen years after his original study. *Chan Kom,* published in 1934, had been undertaken with Alfonso Villa Rojas for the Carnegie Institution, a part of the now classic *The Folk Culture of Yucatan.*

More recently, the Maya have been studied by Charlotte Zimmerman (1969), Villa Rojas (1969), as well as by Strickon (1964), Goldkind (1965), and Avila (1969). A number of the studies done over the years have been coded and indexed by Murdock in the *Human Relations Area File* (See Appendix 2).

2

Vignettes of Nine Key Women

LUZ

Doña Luz, wife of Don Trini, was always a pivotal figure in my trips
to Chan Kom. The first day I went into Chan Kom I hadn't intended
to stay, but Don Trini and his family were so cordial that I decided to
spend a few days there. "Stay with us, Señora," Don Trini had offered.
"Doña Luz will take care of you."

From that first night, Luz became my mentor and my guide to the
Mayan past of Chan Kom. After dinner she invited me to go with her
to see a *loh casa.* I was amazed, not only to be invited to a Mayan
ceremony on my first night in the village, but because in *Chan Kom,
A Mayan Village* I had read:

> At the present time the old ceremony *(u chuyenil na)* that took place on
> such occasions (before a new house is to be occupied) is no longer per-
> formed, principally because most new houses that are built nowadays are
> of masonry.

> (Redfield/Villa Rojas, 1934, p. 146)

Essentially, the ceremony is one of blessing the new house and
ridding it of any evil spirits or winds which it might contain. I readily
accepted her invitation. We walked with several small children to the
edge of town. The stars were bright but it was a very dark night, and
in the distance we saw a light coming from a thatched hut. It was a
beautiful hut, newly made, and the shape and design were just as I had
seen them in pictures of the traditional Mayan dwellings. The timbers
in the corners of the house formed angles—sacred crosses—and
gourds were suspended in these corners with *zaca* (food) for the good

and evil spirits. In the middle of the room a table was fixed up as an altar. The young girls went over to the fire where the women were preparing special small tortillas. Luz and I were given folding chairs, and were later moved to a place just behind the *h-men.* The hens had already been offered and sacrificed, and were being cooked. Everything proceeded very much as I had read in the Redfield description, except that the service was performed by the *h-men* and not the *maestro cantor* (leader of the chants in the Catholic Church). There were cigarettes on the table, also, which Redfield had not mentioned, and men were blowing smoke in the room to dispel the evil winds. I felt awkward sitting in such a conspicuous place, so I moved over to the side in the shadow, away from the center of the activity. At the time I would have given anything to have had a tape recorder, particularly to record the rhythm of the chants which seemed so similar to the chants of the Catholic mass. The combination of the Spanish and Mayan words, the Catholic saints and the Mayan gods, was fascinating. By that time Doña Luz was asleep, nodding in her chair. Even though I wanted to stay longer, her fatigue combined with my embarrassment (the *h-men* kept turning around and asking what I thought of the ceremony) made me suggest that we leave before the *loh casa* was finished. We walked slowly back in the dark, and I went to my room to record my impressions while they were still fresh in my mind.

It is difficult to write about Luz, because she was simply so busy all of the time that I never had enough time to be alone with her. Without her, however, my stays in Chan Kom would have been very different. She gave me information about countless things every day—the animals, food and medicines, customs of the women, the *milpas,* and especially, the Mayan past of Chan Kom. She seemed to be very much in tune with it, and later Alfonso Villa Rojas told me that he thought she still prayed to the sun in the early morning and evening. Luz is the one who introduced me to the whole rhythm of life in Chan Kom—the natural pattern which I soon adopted: rising a little before sunrise, retiring when it got dark to talk with the families sitting peacefully in their hammocks.

In a later conversation, Villa Rojas was surprised to learn that I had been able to communicate with Luz, that she accepted me so quickly. He had not been aware that she could speak much Spanish. I think this is because when Don Trini is around, he answers almost all questions directed at Luz, and seldom lets her speak for herself. This was another reason I found it difficult to have extended conversations with her. By my third trip to the village, I realized that Luz's Spanish was not as good as I had thought it was, but that she was such a discerning, empathetic person that she always seemed to know what I was saying. It was not pretence out of courtesy, as I often felt was true of Ana, who would say she understood when I was sure she did not. Luz simply intuited what I was saying to her.

I learned very little about her life before she came to Chan Kom. She was born in Tekom where her parents and grandparents had been born before her. The eldest of five children, she soon had to take responsibility for her two sisters and her brother since her mother died when she was quite young. Her father, who made *milpa* for his living, married again and had a little girl by that marriage. Luz almost never talks about her mother, but she remembers her grandmother well and says that she taught Luz to make tortillas when she was seven years old. I learned nothing about her life from age seven to nineteen except for such small things as how she loved to dance the *jarana* at fiestas. She is mentioned in Don Trini's autobiography as "the young lady from Tekom":

> . . . I got a young lady of Tecom . . . to work in my house. But soon there was a difficulty with my wife, and I found myself obliged to go with the girl to Merida. I was there six days in a hotel and ten days in the house of Don Dolores Presquel. I went with the girl to talk with the *Liga Central,* and they gave me assurances, and transportation to return to my village.
> . . . Having received a communication from the Presidente Municipal of Cuncunul in which he summoned me to appear in connection with a complaint lodged against me by my mother-in-law and my wife, I answered the Presidente: 'Tell my mother-in-law and my wife that I am working at home as before, and that until the end of my life I will continue to live properly with my wife, but in case any action is taken against me, I will sign nothing in the matter. I send a mule for her to use in returning, in charge of the bearer, whom I have paid. . .'
>
> (Redfield/Villa Rojas, 1934, p. 226)

This is Don Trini's account, which, as the authors mention in introducing it, is not objective. I am not certain about his relationship with Luz at the time, but he did tell me during one of my visits that after reading the Bible he had decided that a man could have two wives if he wished because the ancients had done it. At that time, two other men in the community had already taken second wives. At any rate, I have heard various accounts of how the living arrangements were made for the two "wives." Apparently they all lived together in the one house for a while; then Hilaria moved to the ranch at Tinicacaap, and Luz stayed to take care of the house in Chan Kom. According to Victoria and others, Don Trini severely mistreated both Luz and Hilaria, and often "hit Hilaria until she bled." The men did not mention this, but the women did; Victoria told me that she left their house because, "I could not stand to see him mistreat my mother-in-law so." After a while, Hilaria's arthritis got so bad that she could barely move, and Don Trini brought her back to the house in Chan Kom where Luz took care of her. I do not know whether they became friends then, but on my November visit I learned that Luz and her sister had sung the mass for Hilaria during the *Finados* after All Saints and All Souls.

Doña Luz is small, bright and quick witted. She is almost as strong and wiry as Gabriela, amazing for someone her age. Sometimes when she is tired or cross, the lines in her face deepen and she appears almost ugly; but when she is excited about something or enthusiastic her face lights up, her eyes shine, and she seems pretty. Luz is a quiet person, changeable, and I found it really difficult to understand her completely. From time to time she is moody and withdrawn, at others, completely open and cheerful. She is always extremely energetic. Her movements are deft and she wastes little energy; she always seems to know where she is going.

One night, as we sat in the courtyard just before sunset, Luz told me to look at the profile of the turkeys against the sky.

> Each turkey has his own stone on the wall. . . . I can look at their profiles and know they are all there. If one is eaten or sold, its place stays empty until a baby turkey grows up and takes one of the empty stones. You know, if they sleep with the chickens they get sore feet and die. They eat *zacate*, the wild grass in the plaza, but they always come home for their *masa* and water.

Luz seems especially fond of her pigs, who are the most spoiled, most demanding animals I have ever seen. They come in to eat at certain times during the day, and if their food is not ready they make a horrible racket. Luz told me, "If you don't have their food and water ready for them they run away from you." Her favorite is a white pig named Rosa whom she feeds specially in a little carved out stone. All the animals eat outside the thatched hut on the rocky ground that surrounds it. The courtyard is strangely clean, scattered with bits of paper and cloth, but no excrement in spite of the turkeys, chickens, dogs, pigs, cats and babies. Somehow everyone knows just when to come into the thatched hut for tidbits. There was a strange dancing order: people and animals moving in and out, perhaps hitting at each other or stepping on each other, but all in all a peaceful kingdom.

The hut of Luz and Trini is between two masonry buildings, one owned by Don Trini and one by a daughter. It is an old hut, which gave me a happy, cozy feeling. It always seemed to be the center of some activity. On the ceiling are streamers of soot from the fire hanging down like black mobiles. It is fairly small; at one end is the kitchen area run by Doña Luz. There is the typical three-stone hearth, with an iron *comal* where tortillas are cooked. Behind the hearth are earthen jugs for the many necessary pails of water. There is also a sideboard of small logs held up by forked saplings, which is always covered with many jugs, pots and pails. It seems to be in a clutter, but Luz always knows where everything is. Around the hearth there also are hanging baskets of dried herbs and spices, which she chooses from judiciously while cooking. The table where the tortillas are made is a large circular piece of mahogany, with another smaller circle jutting out from one side where the *masa* is put. The three legs are removed daily for the scrubbing down of the table with ashes and *zocil* (a leaf that very much resembles brillo), after which it is set on its side to drain. There is another small table at Luz's that is used either as a stool or a place for the children to eat. The women eat at the table where they make tortillas, sitting on logs smoothly polished from constant use. The men usually eat at a regular table, using hand-made straight-backed chairs. At the back of the hut is an area about the size of a shower stall that is set out from the oval of the hut; this is where the family bathes. One at a time they sit with a pail of water beside them on a chair or a stool, with their feet on a stone to keep them from getting muddied. The rest of the hut is the living and sleeping area, where the hammocks are pulled down for sleeping or as extra chairs for guests, and thrown up over the rafters during the day. Luz has complete charge of the kitchen where she and Don Trini, Don Trini's son Antonio and his family, her only son by Don Trini, Jorge, and his wife and son, eat. It is also a kind of restaurant for any visitors who happen to be in town. There are always quite a few people to keep fed. Flora (Antonio's wife), her two girls, and Ana help out washing, cleaning, and preparing food, but it is clear that Luz is the one who runs things and does much of the work.

Doña Luz plays many roles in Chan Kom. She manages Don Trini's large family, is an affectionate grandmother and in many cases seems to be accepted both as mother and grandmother by many of the small children; she is well known for her abilities in making the famous *relleno negro,* for burning chiles, and for other traditional Mayan dishes. Most important for many of the people, she is a very good *yerbatero,* one who heals with herbs. Almost every morning before breakfast she held "office hours" in her kitchen. Not only did people from Chan Kom come but also families from the outlying *rancherias* and sometimes people from other villages. She would consult carefully with each of them and give them one herb or another with instructions on how to administer it. She never told them what kind of herbs they were, though. Don Trini told me, "You can't know the name of the medicine or it won't work."

When I mentioned Geronimo to her she remembered him immediately. She told me that she was just then treating another little boy who had Geronimo's illness.

I asked Luz one day if she had shared her herbal medicine lore with Miss MacKay, a nurse who had come in the thirties to Chan Kom as a member of the Carnegie expedition at Chichen Itza. She told me that she remembered Señorita MacKay and how she loved to dance, but that they had never talked about her medicines. Miss MacKay had not asked her, she said. Don Trini told me, however, that he had gone over to Chichen Itza and talked with Miss MacKay and the doctors there about Luz's cures. He told me that there were many good *curanderas* in Tekom and that Luz had learned from them when she was a child.

On my third trip to Chan Kom, I had become very ill in Chichen Itza and was still sick when I arrived. I was so weak that I was not sure I could make it all the way on the long walk in, and once there I was certainly too sick to leave. As soon as I arrived I went to see Luz and told her, "Doctora Luz, I know you can make me well and keep me well. I have never been sick in Chan Kom." And I explained my symptoms to her. She was pleased that I had come to her, and immediately brewed me some herb tea. She put me on a restricted diet and fed me certain herbs and herb teas. Don Trini insisted that I take *mexiforma,* too, and soon I was feeling better.

In a few days, Luz invited me to come *leñar* (get fire wood) with her. I knew that it was on these trips to the forest that she would gather the roots and leaves for her herbal medicines, so I readily accepted. After her reminder about the *garapatas* (chiggers), I covered myself with insect repellent. Luz put on her old ragged yellow *huipil,* which she always wore on these trips to the woods. I had never really understood why the women did not seem to mind going to the woods; the immense loads of firewood they brought back looked painful to carry on their tump lines, their foreheads straining against the rope. The little children also seemed to love going to the woods with Luz. The trip was a mixture of work and play; only Rudolfo turned back sulking when she told him that if he came he had to bring his tump line and help. When we got to the forest I understood why Jorge had told me that Luz likes to get wood. The woods were beautiful and quiet; secret paths led off in all directions, and Luz seemed to feel completely at home there. A

Mayan friend, wife of a gynecologist working near by, told me later that
when the women go to *leñar* it is an outing—a group experience. "The
women love it," she said. "They are free in the woods." In addition
to collecting wood, Luz gathered all the different kinds of flowers,
plants and roots in her *sabucan* (shoulder bag made of henequen
fibre). She seemed to know exactly what she was looking for and where
it would be found, and carried a short machete with her to cut off the
leaves and roots she wanted. On our way back from the woods, we took
a detour and went down the road to the cemetery. A waist high stone
wall surrounded the stark field, and at the east end was a small
thatched *oratorio* (place to pray). Luz told me that there had been a
Mayan *oratorio* next to the *cenote,* a large one of stone, but that they
had dismantled it and had used the stones to build the Catholic and
Protestant churches. It was difficult to tell how many had been buried
there, since there were few markers. To the right of the *oratorio* I saw
the largest raised stone vault in the cemetery. Luz told me that it
belonged to Doña Hilaria.

The day we had gone to *leñar* was my last day in Chan Kom that
summer. When we got back, Luz started explaining the uses for the
different herbs she would rub and mix together. "This is for *ojo*," she
said. This meant, literally, "eye," and I thought that she meant it was
an eyewash of some kind. But she and Ana who had joined us both
laughed at the idea of putting medicine in one's eye. "No, just bathe
the baby," she said. Ana added, "If a visitor comes on a journey and
is hungry and looks at the baby, the baby gets sick and has diarrhea."
"Oh, *mal de ojo* (evil eye)," I said. "I know about that. I was afraid my
blue eyes might make someone sick when I came." There was great
laughter at this too, since the beliefs about the *mal de ojo* are quite
different here than those I remembered from other parts of Mexico.
"Not the color, Señora," Luz laughed. "It's the hunger that makes the
baby sick, and this herb will make him well." She made up little packets
of the various herbs for me. Some of them are as follows:

X-ton (or tun) Cash.. children's diarrhea

Hojo de Aguacate .... sore mouth (boil)
(Ana told me that the tree dies if its leaves are used for medicine and there
are few avocado trees in Chan Kom.)

X-pocim (or pucim)... diarrhea or stomach ache
(grind, strain, mix with sugar)

Flor de San Diego ....sore mouth (use root)

X-shone .... mouth rinse and baths (leaf)
A purgative also for redmouth (root-peel and boil)

When I discussed these things with a nurse in Xochenpich, she told me that many of the ailments mentioned were caused by vitamin deficiencies.

Luz seems totally related to everything around her. She understands nature—she knows how to use it to cure people—and she lives in a world where everything is explicable to her in one way or another. I remember that the first night I spent at Victoria's I was awakened in the middle of the night by a funny clicking sound. I told Luz about it the next day and also said that I had gotten out of my hammock twice to see what it was. Even with my flashlight I had not been able to see anything. Luz was disturbed. "It's the scorpions and spiders that made that noise, Señora, to get you out of bed so they can bite you. You must be careful." I had a window which overlooks the plaza, and Ana asked me if I had left it open. I had. "Perhaps it was a *murcielgo* (bat) from the *cenote*. Sometimes they fly in at the windows." Earlier that week we had killed three scorpions, one of them in Luz's house right by the hearth where she makes tortillas, one in Gabriela's house, and one in my former room, all in the same day. The scorpions, big red ones, had frightened me badly because I almost died from a scorpion bite one time, but Luz did not seem to be at all afraid. She calmly killed them. Other bugs frightened her inexplicably. Later that same day I saw a praying mantis in the kitchen. I find them beautiful, and had always assumed that they were harmless, but Luz was terrified. Another time, in her garden, she found green caterpillars on her cabbage. She knocked them off with a stick, all the while screaming like a girl who has seen a mouse in a Victorian novel.

As I was preparing to leave in the late afternoon a storm began, a thunder storm with great bolts of lightning. "You can't go, Señora; the *chac-chaac* is saying so. The gods are telling you, Señora, you must not go." Greatly concerned, Doña Luz had come up to my little room at Victoria's. I explained that I had to leave then because a truck would be waiting to take me to Mérida, and that I had a plane to catch. But she would not listen. She could not understand my timetable, but she could understand the voice of the gods. Many people in Chan Kom cannot understand why anyone would want to make a trip in the afternoon; they much prefer to get up before dawn and leave. It was hard to explain the "unnatural outside rhythm" of my life while in Chan Kom. But I was very happy and touched by the warmth with which Luz hugged me goodbye. Her son, Jorge, made the three-hour trip in the rain with me. There was one horse between us, and a duffle bag wrapped in a plastic sheet held my camera, tape-recorder, and clothing. Nothing I could do or say would make him ride part of the way or even put some of the baggage on the horse. He carried everything on a tump line, sloshing through the mud.

Jorge is one of the kindest, most intelligent men in Chan Kom. Among the little children, he is everyone's favorite uncle. He is in charge of the *Banda Universal de Chan Kom* (one of the village bands), and everyone seems to have a great deal of respect for him. And more than anything else, it is Don Trini's apparent love for Jorge and his little grandson, Rudolfo, that leads me to believe that he considers Luz his wife, despite what he wrote in his diary. As we waited together for the truck to come, Jorge told me that the people of Chan Kom would always look forward to seeing me, and that in his family especially I had become like one of them—a sister. I was delighted to have been so warmly accepted.

My last trip to Chan Kom was a confusing one. The highway was just being completed, it was almost fiesta time, and everything seemed to have changed. Doña Luz' kitchen, before so neat and orderly, was in a mess. Don Trini was away in Mérida, so everything was being arranged and rearranged. Mario was bringing in new timbers for building. Things were being cleaned; dresses and *huipiles* were being brought out and tried on in great disorder. That evening Luz invited me and my field assistant, Susan Roberts, to go with her to the *Pib* ceremony. This included the making of the famous *relleno negro,* for which purpose she had been "lent" to Don Catalino, the bonesetter. We were very excited. When we arrived Luz left us and began what looked like a very difficult job of getting everything ready for the actual making of the *Pib*. Finally, she brought a concoction of black spices to add to three large kettles in which the *relleno negro* was to be made. The kettles had been set into the red earth, surrounded with heated rocks. One contained a scrawny chicken, one a mixture of pork and chicken meat, and one a large pig's head, with the ears or nose occasionally bubbling to the top. We stood around with other people and watched her flavor the pots carefully with herbs, onions, and various other ingredients: tasting, stirring, adding pinches of this and that, stirring some more. Everyone was solemn. After she was through, the three men there added specially ground *masa* to the mixtures. Each man was assigned one pot to stir carefully and thoroughly "so that the masa will not lump." The pots were then buried in the hot stones and ashes and covered, first with poles which had been cut to the exact size needed, then with banana stalks, and finally with dirt. There they would cook all night. We were invited to return the next day at 8:00, and that morning, Luz's job seemed to be less demanding. We finally arrived at the house where the *Pib* was being held at 10:30, but from the activitiy it seemed that we were actually early. After the pots had been dug up, Luz came and scooped out some of the still-boiling liquid in a gourd. An elderly man, the ceremonial leader, took the gourd and put it on a *chuyub* (holder made of henequen), and walked over to the woods nearby where he hung it on a branch as an offering. He said something in Mayan, bowed and moved his hands in prayerlike fashion. It was for the Mayan gods, Luz explained, urging, "Take a picture, take a picture." In the following ceremonies of drinking rum with coke after the offerings, Luz's only job seemed to be to sit in the corner, pass out bowls of *relleno,* and eat continuously. She sat with her back to the center of the room and ate steadily for at least two hours.

The following day Don Trini returned, very tired, from Mérida. He had brought a gift of perfume for Luz, which was the only thing I ever saw him give to her. Actually, he did not exactly give it to her. When he walked in he put it on the table and then walked out again without a word. After he had gone, Luz smiled delightedly as she opened the perfume and began to splash it vigorously under her arms. She looked very happy and she offered me some.

That afternoon Susan and I came to supper to find Don Trini talking with Alvaro, Jorge, Rufino, and another member of the town council. They spoke in Mayan so I did not know what they were saying, but the words sounded angry. After a while the men left without saying good-bye. Earlier there had been haggling over the price of one of Luz's turkeys—all of that conversation I understood was "eighty pesos!" "No, sixty!" back and forth, with the huge black turkey being poked and prodded in the middle of the room. Don Trini told us that he was angry at them for not taking the responsibility on themselves for planning the governor's breakfast. They expected Doña Luz to do it all. "Victoria (Alvaro's wife) doesn't want to lose a day of sewing," he said. "And Jorge has someone working for him so he will lose two days." This was the first time I had seen Don Trini show real consideration for Luz. I always found it difficult to assess their relationship. In one of our conversations he told me that Luz had come to his house as a servant, and that was all she was to him. But I reminded him that I had read his autobiography, and that he had told me himself that they had been married by the church after Hilaria died. They were not "civilly" married, but I wonder if this was so that Luz could keep her share of *ejido* land which was pooled by the Mecab *sociedad* of which she was a member. Don Trini answered me vaguely. I wondered if he was merely tired, if his age was beginning to tell in a loss of memory, or if, possibly, I was treading on private information. I do not believe that he regards Luz as a mere servant, partly, as I have said before, because of his demonstrated affection for Jorge and Rudolfo. He is obviously proud of his son.

But there are negative things too. For example, Don Trini is fond of talking about what a *vaquera* (cowboy's girl) Hilaria was, and about the dances they used to go to. He refuses to dance with Luz. Once when I was replaying a recording of Don Trini's harmonica music, she began to dance in the kitchen, full of spontaneity and joy. Then Don Trini took over. He did not dance with Luz, but stood in front of her, hiked his pants up above his knees, unbuckled his *huaraches* and began to dance to his own music, alone.

Although Don Trini often ignores her and seems to dominate her a good deal of the time, Luz is a strong figure. She is wise, and many people respect her judgment, not only in matters of herbal lore, but in family affairs as well. She seems to be at the heart of most of the activity of Chan Kom—quiet, observing, aware.

ANA

When I arrived in Chan Kom, one of the first things Don Trini took me to see was the new school. On our way there, we passed a crumbling red building where I could hear a band practicing. We paused outside the door, and there in the middle of the room we saw a little boy dancing, very joyful and unselfconscious. In the far corner of the room the band was playing. In a few minutes, a young woman walked into the room with some corn to grind in the *molino* on the other side of the room. She smiled at the little boy and he ran over to hug her. This was Ana. She could have walked out of a Bonampak mural; she was so much like the beautiful women one sees portrayed in the ancient Mayan glyphs. Her black hair was pulled up in a knot on her head, and her *huipil* was spotless. I went in to record some of the band's music, and learned that the leader of the *Banda Universal de Chan Kom* is Ana's husband, Jorge, and the little dancing boy is her only child, Rudolfo.

I met them again that day in Don Trini's compound where they eat two and sometimes all of their meals each day. Jorge is Don Trini's only son by Doña Luz, and is very close to his mother. He seems to consult her on most matters of importance, and often goes over to visit her by himself during the day. The cooking arrangement pleases Ana, because it means that she needs to keep only a small kitchen in her own house and it spares her from much of the heavy work. Ana told me that it costs "a little, no more," to feed the three of them. It averages about five pesos a day, and occasionally Ana brings Doña Luz extra eggs, or tomatoes and hot chiles from her own garden.

The families seem to enjoy eating together, and Don Trini likes having his grandchildren about him. "They are my wealth," he said to me as the little boys came up to kiss him goodnight, "the future of Chan Kom."

It seems to me impossible to discuss the lives of Don Trini's children without emphasizing the influence of Don Trini himself at the center of it all. From one point of view he is a selfless man, a strong upholder of the patriarchal tradition, whose main interest is in establishing Chan Kom as an important village. On the other hand, he can be seen as cruel, even ruthless, and he has tried at every turn to subordinate the wishes of his wives and children to his own. But perhaps he sees those as wishes for the good of the community; I feel sometimes that he cannot separate his personal hopes from his hopes for Chan Kom. However, I have been told by Victoria and Anita that he used to beat his first wife until she bled, and beat Doña Luz also when he was younger. More unfortunate than this, he forced three of his older children to marry their first cousins: I think this was to keep them in Chan Kom. This went against ancient proscriptions about such marriages, and was done against the counsel of the priest and over strong objections from the *h-men*. All three families suffered terribly for this. The deaths and the sickness, both physical and mental, were interpreted by the people of Chan Kom as retribution for the sins of intermarriage.

I was also told that before Jorge knew Ana, he had been in love with one of the school teachers and she with him, but that Don Trini had forbidden him to marry her because she was dark. When I asked Don Trini about this later he spoke hesitatingly, and said that he was ashamed that color was so important to him. He knew that the teacher was intelligent and would probably have made Jorge a good wife, but he was thinking about his future grandchildren. "The world is kinder to white-skinned people," he said, and told me that he believes the white race to be the race of leaders. He has tried to make all his sons marry light-skinned, beautiful women, as these are qualities that he feels the world prizes.

Jorge had obeyed his father, and told me that when he saw how beautiful Ana was that he was glad Don Trini had not let him marry before. He told me how much he loved Ana, and was eager to show me their wedding pictures. Ana was working at her father's ranch in Canca Un when Jorge first met her. He used to stop there for water on his way to Valladolid to arrange cattle deals for his father. He told me later that Ana had turned down several others suitors before he met her, but when I asked Ana about it she just laughed and giggled like a young girl.

Ana told me earlier that the happiest time in her life had been the months before Rudolfo was born. She said that she and Jorge had been delighted to have a child coming, and were very content and loving with one another. They seem to be a very close, loving family. Jorge is openly affectionate with Rudolfo, even more than most of the men in Chan Kom, who are unusually tender with their children. He is not demonstrative with Ana at all, however, at least while I'm around. In fact, in all of Chan Kom I never saw a husband and wife touching, or even looking at one another affectionately. But his love for Ana is apparent. I still remember the expression on his face as we stood by the well, listening to the tapes of Ana singing being played back to him. She has a child's small soft voice, and is herself at times very trusting, shy, and childlike.

Ana left four younger brothers and sisters behind in Canca Un when she married. She told me that her favorite memories of childhood were of making little things out of sticks and leaves and mud—both she and Rudolfo are very artistically inclined—or of playing house with her sisters. The boys had to play apart from them and would go off to pretend making *milpa* or other things in imitation of their fathers. "We would make little tortillas with herbs and pretend to eat them and say we were making supper just like Mama. Or we'd pretend to make novenas like Papa," she said. Ana told me she was a happy little girl, and usually good—except sometimes at school.

> If you didn't turn in your letters the teacher would make you bend over and hit you with a stick. When you were tired of this you learned to turn in your letters. And if your Mama found out you hadn't done the work, she would spank you again, and maybe your father too.

Her family was a close, religious one, *"muy catolica"* she told me, and that is probably why these two qualities seem to dominate in Ana. She is feminine and motherly, and also very religious. The gods she believes in are a mixture of Mayan and Catholic deities, and when I asked her if she thought there was any difference between the kinds of gods, she did not seem to understand the question. Don Trini had told me earlier that he thought the Mayan gods were rather like Catholic apostles, but Ana's beliefs are much more organic. At home she keeps an orange-colored Mayan cross, and at the same time she goes often to church for the novenas. She believes in the Christian Savior, and also in the many gods of the wells, the fields, bees, houses, and forests. They are vividly real for her. She told me that the sickness in her legs was caused by the evil winds, "the universal bringers of disease," as Redfield says. "They always come from the East," Ana told me, and many are believed to come from the *cenotes* which are, she says, somehow connected to the sea.

Ana had been sick for some time with pains in her leg, and the day before I arrived on my second visit she had been given a treatment by one of the *h-men*. For more than twelve days she had been so ill that she could leave her hammock only with great difficulty. Her knee was so swollen that she could scarcely bend it. She awoke one morning with it swollen, she said, without having fallen or having hurt herself in any way. She also had a high fever, and when I saw her she still had a bad fever blister on her lower lip. Doña Luz, who is a respected *curandera,* had given her treatments and massage but with no results. So on Friday they called in the *h-men* to give her a treatment called *"casap ik"* which is a treatment for the evil winds, the *mal aires* or *vientos maleficos.* The service was performed in Ana's house with Doña Luz and Ana's mother, who had come from Evitum with Ana's younger sister. A black chicken had been provided, and amid chanting the *h-men* instructed his assistant to carry it around Ana's hammock nine times, holding the beak in his hand. The ninth time around, he held the chicken over Ana's head, and without any apparent violence, the chicken died. It was plucked and then cooked by the *h-men* in a fire which was prepared in the corner. He put herbs and other special ingredients into it, and the women made thirteen special small tortillas to be eaten by the evil spirits. In the final part of the ceremony, the *h-men* pricked Ana's knee with the fangs of a rattlesnake, to let out the evil winds. In the meantime, a table was prepared on which the family cross—a brilliant orange one about a foot high—was placed on a stand. It was put in the middle of the thatched hut between the two main hammocks. The bowl filled with the cooked chicken was later placed in front of this. A chair was put in front of the table, and four bottles of anise were set down, one for each corner. Ana was undressed, washed, and given fresh clothes to wear while her old ones were being boiled to rid them of the evil winds. Then she sat down in the chair, and the family members and the *h-men* began to eat the chicken after an offering had been made to the Mayan gods. Ana told me that the next day she felt much better and was able to walk around. That was the day I came back into the village, and Ana was looking healthier. She was dressed in clean clothes and was reading a book, *El Eterno Amor, Hogar,* (Home, the Eternal Love), with a poem in front which read: "My home is the best nest for love, for me to live and rest in."

It is hard for Ana to be sick and immobilized, because she loves taking care of her house and animals and garden. Four years ago Jorge bought the house where they are now living from one of the Protestant founding families for 4,000 pesos. It has fruit trees, coconut palms, Ana's garden, which is built up on sticks so the animals cannot get into it, the beginnings of a stable, and a very deep well. Jorge earned this money by tending his cattle in the fields, and by playing with the band. He works as a *vaquero* with his half-brother Antonio for his father and brothers on the family cooperative cattle ranch. They are paid by the others to take care of the cattle; since they share this work each has time to do other things to make money, such as work on the highway and play in the band. Ana has a separate income of her own, and the more I talked with her, the more I was impressed with the care she took in running her own business matters. She told me exactly how much money she earns from her embroidery, hammock-making, raising turkeys, chickens, and pigs, and selling eggs and vegetables from her garden. She also operates one of the four gasoline-powered mills in Chan Kom, the *molino de nixtamal.* The mill is jointly owned by Jorge, Don Trini and Antonio. They all get a share of the profits, and Ana gets paid for operating it. This money is her own. Jorge gives her money for food, although sometimes she pays for it. The rest she saves. Ana has more time to do these things than most of the women in Chan Kom because she has only one child. It has been four years since Rudolfo's birth, so I asked Ana if she wants ever to have more children. She laughed and said,"Who knows? It means more work. You have to be with them at all hours, and they cry and waste your time." Perhaps she has learned this lesson watching the hard lives of most of the other women in Chan Kom with their never ending succession of children.

Ana is kept very busy with Rudolfo, who is bright and demands much of her attention, and with all of her work. But she does all these things at a quiet pace. She is a serene woman, and lives tranquilly, without hurry. Her house is always clean and orderly; her businesses run smoothly. I go by her house often and find her sewing, reading, or talking with Rudolfo and telling him stories. Even in running her *molino,* with people in and out from 4:30 in the morning until six at night with only an afternoon break, she manages as if she were receiving callers, always relaxed and gracious. She seems to be a part of everything around her and has a respect and love for wild things, growing things, animals. All the songs she sings on the tape I have of her are about animals: the little girl-rat, the girl who is raising a pheasant, the white horse. There is a sense of great peace about her.

The one ambition Ana seems to have is shared by Jorge: to send Rudolfo to school in Mérida where Jorge was forbidden to go by Don Trini. They are even considering moving there for the time that he would be in school. Rudolfo is quite intelligent, but terribly spoiled and demanding. Ana and Jorge want everything for him. Teachers do not come often to Chan Kom, and when they do their classes are crowded. So when they are there, Ana always makes it a point to ask them to eat with her family so that they can know Rudolfo and he can learn from them. Ana had three years of school, and Jorge perhaps a few more. They hope that if Rudolfo gets a good education he may become a professional, a doctor or perhaps a lawyer.

Unlike some of the people in Chan Kom, Ana and Jorge are looking forward to the road coming in. As Jorge and I walked the three hours out of the village in July through a thunderstorm, I asked him if he was tired of living there. "Have you ever thought about leaving Chan Kom?" "Just in the past I thought about it, but now with the road coming, why should I ever want to leave?" The road will mean more jobs for Jorge's band, more business in general for Chan Kom. And although Ana is shy in some ways, she loves to see new people, to talk and go to fiestas. She told me that she does not see the coming of the road as destructive, but rather as something that will make their lives happier and more interesting.

At sunset, the bells ring from the church. At this time Ana is usually in her house with Rudolfo, sitting peacefully. She goes to the novenas at night. When Jorge comes home they go to dinner at Don Trini's house and sit talking quietly in their hammocks. Her home, her family, her religion—these are the fixed things in Ana's life.

On the day that I was to leave after my second visit to Chan Kom, two things happened concerning Ana which disturbed me very much. That morning I went to breakfast at Don Trini's house and found that Jorge had already eaten and left. This was unusual since we always breakfasted together, and I knew that this had something to do with my inviting Ana to drive with me to the clinic in Xochenpich on my way back. First one leg had gotten worse again, then the other, and we were all worried about her. But Jorge seemed to be unsure that she should go to a doctor, and the night before he was in deep conversation with his mother throughout the meal, all in Mayan, so I had no idea what they were saying. They kept glancing at me though, so I supposed that it concerned my offer. Ana confirmed this later on, saying that Jorge had a job with the band that night, and did not want to leave the house with nobody there. But it was more than that. He believed that the *h-men* could cure her, and did not trust doctors. Also, I thought, perhaps he did not want her to go all that way with only me to accompany her. The only thing I could do was to leave a card with the name of the doctor with her, so that she would have some introduction if she should go there later on. But I worried that I might have caused trouble between Ana and Jorge.

In the course of talking with Ana that day about the customs among women about menstruation, I asked her if it was taboo to have sexual relations during the menstrual period. She hesitated for a moment and then seemed quite upset. She told me that she and her husband never slept together any more. "Our hammocks are apart. My husband's hammock is apart from mine, apart from the boy's hammock." It has been four years since Rudolfo's birth, and she said they have not had intercourse in that time. I asked her if they did not want to sleep together, and she said that neither she nor he did. He never said anything about it. I learned then that she had been very sick with Rudolfo, was in labor for twenty-four hours, and had almost died. In a broken voice she told me that it is common for women to die in childbirth, and that their husbands come and say, "Is it because of me that you are dying? And they cry because she is dying. And many die."

I did not know how Ana felt about sex. Some of the women in Chan Kom seem to regard it as unclean: *porquerias* (lit., piggish behavior, filthy or dirty, a naughty act), one of them called it. But it seemed to me that this abstention explained why Jorge had been spending more and more time with the pretty girl in the store nearby. So I gave Ana the name of the Mayan doctor in the clinic in Xochenpich who had just returned from a birth control clinic, and urged her to tell Jorge about him so they could go to the clinic together. But as he would not let her go for her illness, it did not seem likely that he would let her go for this either. So I left Chan Kom that time doubly worried about Ana.

The first thing I did on arriving on my third visit was to ask how Ana was. I had paid my compliments to Don Trini, and left my things in the house of Doña Victoria. Doña Luz prepared an egg and some tortillas, and Jorge joined us in her kitchen greeting me warmly. "I knew you were coming today, Señora, because this morning Ana was weaving your colors into the hammock." He invited me to go see her at his house, and there on the hammock frame was a blue design of the dress I had worn all during my last visit, being woven into the white. "I knew you were coming, Señora," she said as she greeted me happily. Ana seemed quite healthy, and she and Jorge were very relieved. She was anxious to tell me what had happened. "After you left I kept dreaming about you at night, for an entire week. You were in the road, showing me the way. And the final day, you came to the turn in the road, and pointed the way to the clinic." At the end of the week she had told Jorge that if he would not take her to the clinic, she would take her own money and go without him. Her mother had come down to help take care of her and was encouraging her to go; they could go in together. Jorge was against it, and if I understood correctly, his mother Luz was too. Ana insisted, and at the end of two weeks, she, her mother, Jorge, and Rudolfo went to Xochenpich. She stayed there for two weeks, and Jorge came to visit her every third day. The people in the clinic were very kind to her and she was delighted with the treatment she received. She took the card introducing her to the doctor, which had gotten her immediate attention, much to her surprise and pleasure.

> When we arrived there were lots of people waiting in the room, but when I showed the card they brought me in immediately. Two nurses gave me *inyecciones,* one in my arm and one in my hip—Señora, the needles pass straight into the veins!—gave me some medicine to take, a place to stay, and in a little while I was feeling better.

I found out that not only was this the first time Ana had been to a hospital, it was the first time a doctor had given her injections. But she said she was not afraid. They gave her medicine to calm the pain, and other medications, as I later learned, for "arthritis aggravated by an acute vitamin deficiency," and let her stay in one of the little thatched houses by the clinic. Jorge was so happy she was well that he even visited the Protestant *culto* (chapel) across from the clinc to make an offering and give thanks.

During my early morning breakfast at Luz's, I had more time than usual to talk with Jorge, who was getting ready to go to Tini Ca Caap. This is the ranch where the cattle belonging to Don Trini and his family are kept in a *sociedad.* Jorge was talking enthusiastically about his first meeting with Ana. He seemed especially proud that Ana had turned down the other young men who had approached her father about the possibility of marrying her. There was a great feeling of family as he invited me and my field assistant, Susan Roberts, to go over to his house and do our washing at his well.

Ana showed me how she did her laundry, using the ashes from the hearth in the first scrubbing in the long wash trough under the lean-to beside the well. The trough is slanted so that the soapy, ashy water stays at one end, and the clothes are pushed to the other end as they are scrubbed. A pail of water, freshly drawn, was beside us, and we rinsed with a gourd so the least amount of water would be wasted. After hanging our laundry on the clothes line, Ana showed me how to hold the clothes without a clothespin, by pushing the fabric between the two strands of the *soga* (line). The sun was hot, and we were tired. I happily accepted her invitation to come inside the cool thatched hut. Ana proudly showed me the hammock she had just finished, the one I had asked her to make for me. I asked if I could try it out, so she hung it up and we both stretched out in our hammocks.

We talked for a long time about the dreams she had been having. We talked in general about the coming fiesta and the opening of the road. Ana is looking forward to the road being opened. When asked what it will bring and why she is glad, she cannot really answer. "Progress," she says. She sees it as a new source of people and is hopeful of greater income from sales of hammocks and embroidery. I think she anticipates its bringing new life to Chan Kom, more excitement. When I commented on the way she had reprimanded Rudolfo at Luz's earlier in the morning, she smiled but did not reply. In fact, I had been pleased to see her be firm with him for a change, although I think the only reason she did it was because other women were present. That field trip Rudolfo was behaving more and more like a spoiled only child.

As we became more relaxed together, I asked Ana what had been the happiest time in her life. I had asked her this on an earlier visit, and wondered if she would say the same thing. She said, "I'm happy every day. I'm always happy." I reminded her that on my first visit with her she had said that her happiest memories were of the year before Rudolfo was born. Did she feel the same way now? She laughed and did not say anything. I asked her then if she and Jorge had been living with Don Trini at the time. She said yes, but did not amplify. I wonder now why she seemed to grow evasive and silent. I told her of my conversation that morning with Jorge, when he had told me of her previous suitors. He had been so proud that she rejected all of them. I asked her if that was true but she just giggled. "Do you remember the first time you saw Jorge, Ana?" "No." And I asked her if she had ever been hungry or wanted for anything. "No," she said and told me that she had always been happy.

In one of my last talks with Jorge, he told me,

"When Ana had Rudolfo she was very *pálida*—we thought she might die. So we decided to let the midwife fix her so she could not have any more children. She had *verguenza* (was ashamed) and so she did not tell you the first time but that's the way it is.

This news made me feel much better, because of Ana's story that "we have our hammocks apart." It had not seemed possible, watching them, the most affectionate couple in Chan Kom. I also was sad for Ana that she should feel ashamed, and wondered how my questions and remarks about birth control must have affected her. Nonetheless, I still wondered about the situation and about Jorge's motives in telling me this. Doña Concepción, the midwife, had told me earlier that to "fix" a woman so she would not become pregnant again, would be a sin, an interference with God's will. At the time I was not sure that she trusted me; she might have thought that I would mention to the priest what she said. Unfortunately, it was not possible to visit her a second time after the discussion with Jorge, but I plan to do so during my next trip.

Ana's Dreams

Tuesday morning: the week of preparation for the fiesta of the patron saint San Diego de Acala as well as the impending visit of the governor to open the new highway to the village.

Dream # 1

"We were going to a ranch. I don't know what ranch it was. I was going there all by myself, and on the way I met Rudolfo and took him by the hand. At the ranch there was a man I didn't know. Then we came back again. Just as we were getting to the village we met his father, Jorge, by the well[1] there in the *colonia.*[2] He said, 'Where are you coming from?' And we said, 'We are coming from the ranch.' 'What did you see there?' he asked us. 'We only saw a man there.' *(No mas un señor vimos allá)"* Ana laughed and said something I could not quite under-

[1]The well is very deep—it has a great cave at the bottom where semi-precious stones and archeological artifacts have been found—the people in the village say there is a tunnel from the cave which goes toward Chichen Itza, and some say that it goes all the way to Tuluum (on the Carribean).
[2]The *colonia* is a group of isolated thatched huts mixed back into the *solares.* In one of these there is a family where the women have several illegitimate children. Antonio supposedly visits this house often. "Jorge used to go there, and Ana threatened to leave," according to Victoria. It is the only situation I have heard of like this.

stand about Jorge having just come back from his cattle ranch—not the
one she went to in the dream. "I'd never seen this ranch. When we got
back we saw lots of people in the plaza. A truck came and there was
a little boy—about this tall—and the truck kept coming and the little
boy didn't get out of the way. He was killed and crushed into pieces.
'Jesus!' I said. And then I woke up."

I asked her if the little boy had been Rudolfo.

"No, it wasn't Rudolfo. I was holding him by the hand. And I think
that the thing I dreamed is the thing that happened already. The son
of Doña Anita and Demetrio—a piece of a roman candle hit him in the
head. The big children were shooting them off in front of Balerio's
store."

"Was it Emiliano?"

"No it was Fermin. This thing that I dreamed seems to be the thing
that happened already." (Fermin was not killed.)

"And it happened the day after you dreamed it?"

"Yes, the very next day. Who knows how? God shows me these
things. Before things happen, I dream them."

"Like my visit?"

"Yes, I dreamed of that before you came."

"And the dream of going to the clinic?"

"Yes, yes."

And just as we were talking, outside a beer truck hit a woman, not
a little boy, as she was walking into the plaza. We did not know who
she was; the truck driver took her to the hospital. . . .

Dream # 2

"Jorge and I were on a trip, just the three of us. . . . I didn't know the
pueblo we came to. And Then we saw—I don't know what it was—a
thing walking along, but it didn't have any eyes."

"Was it an animal?"

"Yes, it had a body and horns and feet. In the middle of its shoulder
it had *suciedad* (filth, excrement) coming out. It was a different thing.
Who knows where we were going? I didn't know the town we were
going through, and we passed many towns I didn't know. Some days
we saw lots of people and we met them passing by. Thanks be to
God—we had to pass through and I was afraid to. Finally we got to the
end and found a little path—a tiny path with lots of thorns all along
it. We had to follow it. After we had gone a while, we came to a field
and there were San José and María (St. Joseph and the Virgin Mary)

with her Niño Dios (God-Child). There were many people in the field —they were doing evil.[3] We were talking. Thanks be to God that we have come here. I saw many young men whom I did not know, and they said, 'Here comes a señorita.' But I didn't know them and they took me by the hand. I said, 'I am not a señorita. I am a Señora. I was married by my hand *(casado a mi mano)* and I don't deceive *(engaño)* anyone.' Jorge was five meters in front of me. I had Rudolfo by the hand. I looked back to make sure he was still there. I met an older man—older than Don Pasqual—but I didn't know him. He said that the young men wanted me to stay, but I couldn't stay because it wasn't my village. I had Rudolfo by one hand, and in the other I had my hammock woven with flower patterns. He said the flowers were the virtue that I have. He wanted to buy the hammock and have me show him how to weave one.[4] I said, 'I made my own hammock. No one taught me how and I will teach no one. Let anyone who wishes to learn do it alone.' And he grabbed the hammock and said, 'Leave the hammock and we'll let you go.' But I wouldn't let him have it. We waited to se what would happen. We started to walk, with the old man still holding the hammock, and then I woke up. . . . I was sad."

She said she often has dreams of falling out of her hammock.

"When you have a fever, you dream that your house is burning, but it's only your body."

GABRIELA

On my first day in Chan Kom, as I saw the women coming out of their houses looking clean and refreshed, I knew they must have been bathing somewhere. So I asked my hostess, Doña Luz, if I might have a bath. "Of course, Señora," she said, and led me to the nearby house of Doña Gabriela. It is a large masonry house on the plaza, well built, with stenciled drawings on the walls and tile on the floor. I learned later that it had been a demonstration house of the Rural Cultural Mission when they were in Chan Kom, and that Gabriela had inherited it from her husband at his death. Out back there was an extra thatched hut for the chickens, and a room with a cement floor and a drain which was used as a bath. Doña Gabriela and I were introduced by Luz, and

[3]This phrase not completely understood. She said something about *maldades,* which could refer to witchcraft, calling each other bad names, or having illicit sex. . . .
[4]At the time she was teaching Susan Roberts how to weave a hammock—and doing a very bad job of it, as if she did not really want her to learn.

we sat around and talked as Gabriela heated up water in a large pail for my bath. This became part of my daily routine, and I soon got to know Gabriela and her family well.

Many people seem to feel that Doña Gabriela leads one of the hardest lives for a woman in Chan Kom. "She works like a man," Doña Anita told me, and she is much admired for her diligence. Gabriela seems to have much sympathy from the other women because she has no husband to help her with the difficult job of making *milpa*. She owns a fair amount of property in Chan Kom: her large masonry house on a 60x40 lot; a *solar,* or *previo,* of 30 hectares with a wall around it and a deep well; a house on the *solar* property, which she bought for 2,000 pesos—the prettiest, largest thatched hut I have ever seen; and 800 hectares of arable land, also an inheritance from her husband. Despite these holdings, I got the impression that in terms of income Gabriela was not very well off. She was always working, and I wondered if she was making enough to feed and clothe her family. Her children now living with her help in the milpa, except for her twelve-year-old daughter Olivia who was recently "prestado"—lent out to her aunt and uncle for one peso a day. As a widow, Gabriela has a legal right to *ejido* land, 600 *mecates* for herself and 600 for each son. Yet she has not requested it; nor has her father, Don Trini, who is the *Comisario Ejidal,* requested it for her. This land could be used for milpa or, with a fence around it, for cattle. At present, Gabriela and her family are using their own forests for their *milpa,* which seems a shame when there is public land available for them.

Physically, Gabriela is quite different from most of the other women in Chan Kom. Taller and more angular, she seems more athletic and in better health than the others, perhaps because unlike them, she has no excess fat on her body. She is extremely energetic and seems to enjoy heavy, physical work. Her two sons who live with her, Roberto and Guillermo, are industrious, well liked, and often praised. When their grandfather, Don Pascual, mentioned what good *albaniles* (masons) they were, everyone agreed, and said they were equally good as painters and builders. During that visit, they were building an addition to Eduardo's house, and contrary to the statement in *A Village That Chose Progress,* that relatives worked for one another without pay, they were being paid. They were also building a masonry house on the *solar* property in front of the old thatched house, which was in bad disrepair. The boys take after their father's side of the family, being small, thin and wiry, much like the grandfather, Don Pascual. Guillermo, twenty-five, is married and has four little boys. Roberto is only eighteen, and is blonde with strangely yellow cat's eyes. Gabriela's daughters seem listless in comparison. They are built like the rest of the women, stocky, soft and heavy. Carola, fourteen, did little work that I could see, and was childish and giggly compared to other girls her age. Olivia, twelve, was in the unhappy situation of having been loaned out to Doña Victoria and Don Alvaro, her aunt and uncle. Victoria is very strict and works her hard; yet underneath it all she seems affectionate. When Gabriela told me about the arrangement, she seemed to think that it was fortunate for Livi that she had been "prestado."

> She was requested by my brother Alvaro. "I'll treat her like the daughter God gave us and took away. I'll buy her shoes and clothes and earrings," he said. He is buying everything for her now. A peso a day—that's what most people pay. But I told him not to pay me anymore. And she eats and sleeps there. And she's not to come home at all—not even one day a week—not at all. We'll meet sometime at my father's house.

Perhaps Livi is better off materially in Victoria's house, or perhaps Gabriela simply felt that since she was grown it was time that she went to work, but Livi seemed unhappy to me. Often she would come up to my room at Victoria's so that she could look at her house across the way. Sometimes I would find her crying. And one morning I found her in the yard, violently sick to her stomach. I wondered what could be wrong, if it was nerves, homesickness, or the beginning of an illness. Gabriela does care for and worry about Olivia, however it may seem to the contrary.

> But she doesn't know anything at all about life—about men and women and about a woman's life. I must tell her now that she's away. Her menses (mentrual periods) haven't started yet. She might get frightened and with the *fiestas* coming and the *bailes*. . . . She knows I don't want her to go far away. My sister in Merida wanted her to go. But I didn't want her so far away.

Gabriela's youngest daughter is Margarita, nine. Three years after her husband died, Gabriela ran away with a man from another village. She said that she needed a man to help her with her work, and took all her children with her when she went. Later she found out that the man already had a wife and family. Don Trini went to find her and told her to come back. "He was going to take her property," he told me. She didn't know what to do, and so she obeyed her father. Little Margarita was thus raised without a father. She is very much a tomboy. She loves to help her brothers with their masonry work, and enjoys going with her mother to the *milpa*, or to *leñar*. Although she cannot read or write, she does not go to school, and I am not quite sure why

Gabriela does not make her go. She seems to like to play the dunce with other children, to be clowning, and they tease her a lot. I am afraid that it will get to the point where she may not be able to go to school at all without embarrassment. Perhaps Gabriela simply needs her at home to help, although she seems to wander around aimlessly a good deal of the time. She seems lost. And yet she is certainly always there ready to help—to be boosted over a wall to look for something lost, to remove chiggers by candlelight from Luz's back when they came back from gathering wood. She loved to pose with the pet parrot, the still unfeathered baby bird who lives in their kitchen.

As Gabriela and I got to know each other better, the earliest memories which she would talk about were of her mother, Hilaria Puuc Mecab, the first wife of Don Trini. She and her mother were very close, and Gabriela remembers crying when her mother would leave "even for a little while." Her favorite sister was Luisa who took care of her when she was young. Luisa now lives in Mérida, and although Gabriela seldom visits her because it is so far to walk to the bus, she tells me that she thinks of her often. When she can make the trip, she takes her a chicken or something from her garden. Luisa is the sister who offered to take one of Gabriela's children to live with her, and she still hopes one of her sons or daughters will go there for a while. Gabriela is afraid of the city, however; she told me of a little girl who was killed by an automobile there. Aside from this fear, I believe that Gabriela simply does not like to have her children long distances away from her. She told me how distressed she was when her eldest daughter, Cristina, left Chan Kom.

> This boy from another village came to look for a wife and he kept coming to my house because he liked my Cristina, and I wanted her to stay with us because it was so good to have her here after my husband died. And I said he should go away, but he kept coming and he liked her and they got married and they live now in Quintana Roo. The same town as the older Iks—the parents of Victoria and Ampara and Flora. And then she borrowed my six-month old baby (Margarita), and took her with her to the territories. They say they're higher. I got sick and vomited going to find her. We went around and around up to another place I'm sure. I didn't want my daughter to go so far away. But like I said to you, Señora, I will let my daughters marry whomever they want.

She told me that she has no memories of the time when she was a young girl, and did not mention anything about attending school. When she was growing up the Mecab family was living in a thatched hut, farther back in the *solar* than where they now live. She said that her parents took very good care of them. When her marriage was arranged with her cousin German, her mother never let them go out together. "Not even to the plaza, not even to the door!" she said laughingly. But she did not want to be married. "You can scold me, father, but I don't like him," she would say. Nonetheless, when she was fifteen she was married to her first cousin, once removed, son of her uncle Don Pascual. She told me that it took her four months to get used to living with her husband, and all during that time she would cry because, "I wasn't used to being away from my mother." After she had been married to German for a while, she said, an American came and told Don Trini that it was wrong to allow first cousins to marry one another. "Don Trinidad, why did you accept this marriage?" he said. "Your daughter is lost to you now." But my father didn't know about this, and I was in my father's power. . . . We are *puro Mecab, puro Mecab de todo* (pure Mecab on both sides)." Later when a cousin came to ask to be married to Marta, Gabriela's younger sister, Don Trini refused and instead married her at age thirteen to someone she didn't know well. "But we were already married," Gabriela said. And Don Trini told the boy who had wanted to marry Marta that it was wrong, that "It is certain that you will die or be sick or be poor." He added, "May God pardon us because we were like animals." According to Villa Rojas' diary (Redfield/Villa Rojas, 1934, p. 96), at the time of Gabriela's marriage, Don Trini had not been sure whether it was a good thing, but the marriage broker had insisted that it should take place. Don Trini was glad that he had been told it was wrong to marry like that, said Gabriela, because their other cousins had married in the past. Several of these marriages ended tragically; some of the resulting children were either physically handicapped or insane. Gabriela's sister Clara, married to her first cousin Marco, died hemorrhaging and her husband later died also. Gabriela's husband died after their sixth child was born. She feels that her husband's death, and all the other incidents, are punishment for the sin of intermarriage. I don't know what her husband died of, but to this day neither Gabriela nor her eldest son trust the *h-men,* feeling that one was partly responsible for German's death. "Who knows what herbs they might have given him to poison him?" said Gabriela. Even though she had been unhappy to be married when she was, Gabriela had grown to love her husband very much, and she told me that "one forgets only little by little." She remembered the exact date of his death. "It was the 29th of May, Señora," she said, although she laughed when I pressed her for the year. She remembered the dates of several things, including her marriage, but never the year. She was the only woman I talked with who told me that she went often to the cemetery "to see where the person you love is." She told me that although the spirits of the dead don't come back, when you are sleeping the spirit can come in the air and you will dream of the person because his spirit is in the air.

VICTORIA

Doña Victoria is the wife of Alvaro, the only son of Don Trinidad to hold an important political office in Chan Kom. He has been the *presidente municipal* for three terms and has held other offices before that. Victoria was a difficult person for me to get to know. She was always extremely busy at her sewing machine or at her hearth, but once we did become friends, she would often come up to the room in her house where I hung my hammock and slept and talk for hours.

Although in her forties, Victoria is an extremely vigorous person. She is energetic, and works with a diligence which almost approaches compulsiveness. I saw some of the reasons for this emerging as we talked about her childhood. She was the eldest and I asked her what she remembered about her early years:

> There was nothing but work. Ever since I was a little girl, Linda's age, nothing but work and sewing. I wanted to work and make money. I didn't know anything else. . . . There were eight of us (children). . . . I would work from three in the morning until late at night, with a little sleep in between, and then get up again. Until eight in the morning I would be working with the cattle. And after that I would help my mother. And at night I would work on my sewing.

"Why did you work so much?" I asked her. "Because I liked it. I liked money. *Me encantaba mucho.* And I didn't feel like going to sleep."

I learned that she had been quite a tomboy and a tremendous help to her father, who had cried when she married because none of his other children worked the way she did.

> When I was a little girl we were raising pigs and hens. But they didn't belong to us. They belonged to my father. And when it came time to sell them it was hard to remember that they weren't ours. When I was a little girl I was learning to work, to plant and harvest, learning how to take care of the horses, and riding them with my father. I was working hard. And when my brother Martin was still little he was out working with my father too. When I was married my poor father cried because he didn't want me to, because I worked hard and because my brothers were still little. They didn't have anyone to help them and the horses didn't have anyone to take care of them. I knew how to take care of the horses well. My father taught me how to do all of these things. And even now, every time I go to visit him, he still cries. My poor father.

Victoria's marriage was no surprise to her father, however, and
Alvaro had spent two years while wedding gifts were exchanged. Don
Trini had apparently played little part on selecting a wife for Alvaro,
but he had made all of the traditional exchanges with her parents. He
did not help them with the wedding itself, which was apparently the
case with all of his sons except for Jorge. Victoria and Alvaro never had
a "civil" ceremony.

> Don Trini had wanted all of his children to marry relatives to keep all of
> the money in the family and so all would stay here in Chan Kom. But now
> he does not give any to the family.

> I was seventeen when I married. We went first to live with my father-in-law
> and we wanted to make some money. First we were making *arrepitas*
> (sweets) to sell and also cookies. Then Alvaro bought chickens and tur-
> keys. . . . I was selling refreshments at the fiestas and I almost never went
> to the fiestas before that. But I went there to sell things at the stand I had
> on the corner.

Victoria did not like living with Don Trini:

> It was horrible. They fought all the time. He used to beat my poor mother-
> in-law until she bled. He still beats Luz but not so much because he is
> changing. I moved out of his house because I could not stand watching
> him insult my mother-in-law, me, and all women.

After they had been living with Don Trini for a while, an incident
occurred which revealed many things:

> We had a little girl for a while, but she died because we didn't know what
> was wrong with her. She was nine weeks old when she died and I had a
> fever. My father-in-law was bothered with me because I was sick. Ha. And
> what could I do? And he wouldn't give his son any money for medicine.
> *Un poco mal gente mi pobre suegro* (somewhat of a bad person, my poor
> father-in-law). I wasn't important to him.

I learned from Victoria on a later visit to the village that what had
occurred was a confrontation with Don Trini, who had told Alvaro that
he had to leave Victoria because she was sick and all of her hair had
fallen out. "Trini did not want Alvaro to marry me. In fact, when I was
sick he told Alvaro right to my face that he ought to leave me." Alvaro
refused, and took Victoria to live with her father, where he later joined
her:

> We went to live with my poor father, and he used up a lot of money so
> that I could be well again. And I was in pain. The fever would not leave
> me. And my husband left his father to come stay with me. And we stayed
> there together with my poor father. . . . I was cured by *pura medicina,* no
> doctors. I had the fever and they gave me *caliente medicina.* In a year I
> was finally well and we went to work in the bush in Actun.

Victoria has not had a child since that time, although she said that they have spent much money on medicine. I suggested that having had the fever for so long might have made her sterile.

> Who knows? Who knows what happened to me? It is God's will, as God wishes. *Déjalo* (Let it be). . . But after that I wasn't sick again. I was healthy, fat.

Victoria later told me that the time spent in Actun was the happiest of her life:

> We worked there for about ten years. We began to make milpa there, and we raised pigs. We tried to make a little money. We were working together then—even up in the mountains. . . . Those were the happiest times. Alvaro would kill venison up there, and wild turkeys, looking for meat for us to eat. We would gather fruit too. I like fruit very much. And we had around two hundred chickens, too. Many eggs, many chickens. We almost never ate beans.

Her parents were with them in the bush, along with one of Amparo's daughters whom Victoria was teaching to work. Although she and Alvaro have lived in the village for some time now, they may be moving back to the ranch. During my first visit Victoria told me that even though it was Alvaro who was working to bring the road into Chan Kom, he didn't know if he wanted to live there once it had come. Too much noise, too many people. She told me that Alvaro had been responsible for bringing other things to Chan Kom—the school and electricity, even though it lasted for only a few months. She was very excited when she told me about the light. Hers was beautiful, she said, a meter long. She had loved to sew at night, and told me about all of the different kinds of light bulbs.

Victoria told me that Alfonso Villa Rojas was Alvaro's first teacher and the one who told him to study hard and learn how to do things for Chan Kom. I asked her if he got paid for being *presidente municipal.*

> God pays you. That's one of the reasons I say to him please don't be *presidente municipal* any more. But he says that he wants to get the road built before he quits.

Now that the road is completed, it will be interesting to see whether Alvaro leaves office or not.

Victoria's concern for making money seems to influence everything she does and thinks about. I think some of it must originate from the time when she was sick and had no money for medicine so that she had to go back to her father. She told me of another incident, later, when all of her cattle got sick and died. She said that she fell ill then as well.

> One time I had some money saved. And I bought some cattle. They were up in the field, and when they came down to the other fields by the pueblo, they died. They were just about to have calves when they died. Then I got sick. I thought I was dying. Then they told me to leave the other cattle. Forget them—don't worry about them anymore, because of this sickness that is happening to you. Buy some more cows instead. But instead I took the money to lend to Don Bruno (for interest).

Even now, she and Alvaro keep their money separate.

> We each have our own money. We divide everything. He has his cattle, I have mine. Even the ranch—I have part and he has part. Everything that we do, we agree on—down to the money. We are a *sociedad*. We put our things together.

She is very proud of her husband, and told me often how content they are. Once after describing the various intrigues that go on between some of the Mecab men and other women, she said, "Alvaro is not like the other men. He and I have always been happy."

Since Victoria and Alvaro have no children of their own, two sons of Alvaro's brother Antonio and Victoria's sister Flora are living with them as their own. They are Juan, eleven, and Jose, seven. Victoria makes them work hard, but treats them like her own, and she and Alvaro plan to leave everything to them.

> Antonio had no money. Alvaro bought Antonio's clothing, he bought Antonio's shoes. He bought clothing and distributed it. We bought soap and gave it to his wife so that she could wash the clothing because he is a *vaquero* (cowboy). *Así.* This we were very glad to do. And we told Antonio later, because of this we have the right to claim these two little boys. . . Now their father tells them to obey their *padrino*. And I tell them, when we are old and can't work, you are going to manage these things for us. But if they won't obey us, what can I do?

It was difficult to watch her with the children. Juan was bossed around alot and expected to work constantly. José was pushed and shoved and never seemed to be able to do anything right. The saddest, though, was Olivia, their twelve-year-old niece who had been "prestado." She worked very hard all day, and really yearned for some affection, something which I never saw either Victoria or Alvaro show. Juan said he was sad at first at being "regalado", and even ran away once, but feels it is much better now that he has his little brother with him.

One day my field assistant Susan Roberts asked Livi if she would like to help her with her hammock.

"Yes!", she said excitedly.

"How about tomorrow?"

"Oh, I have to draw water, sweep, make tortillas, and do other things for my Tía Victoria."

"When can you help?"

"I never know."

Once, after talking about the "vida regular" a while, I asked Victoria if she thought it was necessary to punish children, to hit them, in order to educate them.

> This is what Alvaro says. We brought the parents here one time to ask permission to educate their children, to teach them to read. Education— this is what we want. But this. A few times, no more, do you punish them by hitting. . . . The first thing I say in the morning (to Juan and José) is, you should obey. And Alvaro tells them this also.

"Do you tell José bedtime stories or sing to him?" I asked.

"What? I tell him he is naughty and to go to bed as soon as he finishes dinner."

I have a feeling that Victoria can have quite a temper when not obeyed, and this may account for Juan's running away once. But she also has a good sense of humor, and I think she does love the boys very much. Her bossiness does not override her concern for the children. She is perhaps just frustrated in some ways. Victoria doesn't seem to raise children with the comfortable ease of the other women. She seems strained and unsure of herself with them. Moreover, she expects them to behave like little adults, and to love work the way she does.

> Do you think Juan and José like it better here or at their old house? I want to get a legal adoption, but I don't think Flora will listen. I'm not sure how Luz feels—I'll have to talk with Antonio. I take care of Juan and José. They are both much stronger than when they came.

Victoria's great energy and belief in the virtues of work, in the importance of diligence, make her a vital person—still curious, still interested. She told me with such eagerness that she had heard that some people could learn to read even when they were old, and that she wanted to learn very much. She told me that Judith, one of Doña Amparo's daughters, is very affectionate towards her, and would come teach her to read when she had time. Victoria is always planning to make up her schooling. Once she overheard me playing a tape with Don Trini speaking (about the Governor's arrival), and heard her name mentioned. Later she asked if he had called her stupid. "Just because I can't read and write I'm not stupid. I just never had a chance to learn. I'm as smart as Don Trini. Now that we have women teachers maybe they will teach me—I'm going to ask them."

Once I asked Victoria which she thought was more important, to be loving or to keep her house clean and orderly. Before I got all the words out of my mouth she said, "to keep on working." After she had heard the whole question, she said it was more important to keep her house orderly and keep a regular life. And she said that we should love God, and then he would bless us and the work we are doing. When I asked her what the worst sins were, naming the ones from the Fromm questionnaire, she said, "Not to work and to steal—it's very bad to live this way." "But which is worse," I asked, "to kill someone and steal from him, or—" She interrupted. "It's all bad. It's bad to kill someone and not to work." That she coupled the two together, I thought, was very telling. "And for a woman, which is the worst sin?" "For a woman, to go with another man isn't good, and also not to work. It isn't good." The only married woman she knew who did this was the bee keeper. She didn't mention any of the women in Chan Kom as being lazy, but she told me that there were places "where they only get up in the morning and go to bed at night—they don't work."

I asked Victoria which was more difficult, the life of a man or a woman. She answered that they were the same, "because the woman, she has to get up early, and start working around three in the morning, and she has to keep on working until about eleven at night." When I was questioning her later about what her mother had told her of the customs of women, her mind was on something else. But what she said was again very revealing. "Did your mother tell you about this?"

VICTORIA: My poor mother? Well, yes. My mother liked for us to learn to work, and when she would hit us she would say, it isn't good not to do anything. And she would hit us and tell us to learn to work. Without it, it isn't possible to live, my poor mother said.

ELMENDORF: If you could start again—if you could be, say, Alexandria's age (Alexandria was sitting beside us), what occupation would you like to have? If you could have whatever job you wanted.

VICTORIA: Ah, I want Alexandria to come and start learning to work with me. It is a good life to work when you are young. To learn when you are little so you'll keep on working when you're grown.

ELMENDORF: What occupation would you like to have, though, if you could choose—a doctor, or a nurse, or a teacher, or a baker. . .

VICTORIA: Working in a bakery is very hard. It tires you out. I did that for a while. I learned how to make those breads. It's a lot of work. You work and the oven you work near is so hot. That's what happened to me. It's easier to sew.

ELMENDORF: Well, wouldn't you like to be, say, a nurse?

VICTORIA: Well, who knows? But they say of nurses that they have no patience. They don't put up with anything, they say. Many people say this.

And with your sewing machine, you can work when you want to. With the machine, if you know how to design the patterns, it is good. There are many girls who have machines, but their sewing isn't as good as mine. They don't know how to design.

I found out that Alexandria was going to learn how to sew from Victoria.

VICTORIA: This one has wanted to sew since she was a little girl. I'm waiting until she gets old enough, and then I'll get another machine and teach her.

I asked Alexandria what she wanted to do when she grew up. She did not answer. "Do you want to get married, or no? She said "no" in a small voice and we all laughed. "But what do you want to do?" She laughed and said "nothing." Doña Victoria laughed and said, "She doesn't want any money." Victoria asked her the question again, in Mayan, and Alexandria said that she wanted to be a seamstress.

"Don't you want to run a beauty salon, or a hotel?" I asked.

"Ah, this too," said Victoria. "This running a beauty salon is a lot of work, they say."

"Well, everything is work," I countered, "But it's important to choose the thing you want to do."

"Yes. That is certain. This designing embroidery—it takes a lot of patience too. That is the hardest thing, learning to design. You shouldn't be afraid, and it will turn out right."

During my last visit, Victoria took Susan Roberts and me to see her *solar* property.

Oh, I am so embarrassed. It is such a mess. We are trying to fix it up little by little. You know we can't do it all at once. . . . Some day I am going to have six great big American pigs. I am going to keep them in here. Everybody's got to have animals. . .

If people keep coming to Chan Kom, I am going to build my house out here near the wall. I will have a much newer kitchen with a corridor to the well. Then I will rent the other house out to people—like a hotel!

FELICIA

Felicia, seventeen, is the daughter of Eduardo, a son of Don Trini, and Amparo, She is the oldest in a family of eight children, four boys and four girls, and has assumed a great deal of responsibility in the life of this close knit group. The family runs a store, and Amparo bakes bread professionally with the help of her children.

For the past eight years, Amparo and Eduardo have been adding rooms to and building a wall around their house. Their goal is to have a room for each child. They also want each child to learn some sort of vocation. Although all of the older children help in the store and bake shop, Felicia takes primary responsibility for the store. She has only had schooling in Chan Kom, but keeps good figures and takes care of such things as the books, purchasing in Mérida, and inventory. The family works cooperatively, with a good deal of affection evident.

While not unhappy in Chan Kom, Felicia wants to go to Mérida as one of her sisters has. With more than a hint of wistfulness she told me the story of her cousin who ran away to the city at midnight during the November fiesta, just four days before her wedding was scheduled:

> She (the cousin) was dancing with her cousins and her future mother-in-law didn't like it. And she could see the way she was going to be treated. She wasn't used to punishments and decided she wouldn't take it from her in-laws. So she ran away to Mérida—she is working in my aunt's store. She likes it. I want to go but my parents won't let me go yet. Later, they say. My sister has gone. So have two of my cousins. They all left during the November Fiesta.

Amparo told me later that:

> We let Adelina go because she didn't know how to do anything and there she would learn and come back and help her father with the store so that Felicia can go.

But even now, with the road and bus service, the girls have not come back, nor have their mothers gone to the city to visit them. In one very real sense Felicia is stuck in Chan Kom. Eduardo is quite close to her, and seemed to become very distraught when she was away. People say he is *muy delicado* (very touchy). Felicia is needed by her parents, both spiritually and economically. Her own feelings are apparent in the definition of love she gave me: "*Amor es vivir juntos y trabajar todos*" (Love is to live together, all working together).

Eduardo is a hard-working man, now striking out on his own to build a secure and independent existence for his family. He told me that he had given up working in his *milpa* and working for his father, Don Trini.

> For ten years I worked for my father. All I earned was my sweat. Sometimes in the *milpa,* with him at the ranch, or doing other things, if I earned any money I had to give it to him. If there was corn, he sold it and took the money. He would buy *solares* and land and cattle and put it in his name and call it his. He said that it was really Don Trini and Sons, but none of the sons have gotten anything. He says that we'll get it when he dies. But will it be left, will we be left?

The first time I met Amparo she told me that she had just cleared 160 pesos in profit in two days selling sweet rolls that she had made. Baking runs in her family it seems. Her brother had come to visit for a few days and had spent a good deal of time teaching her and her daughters new bread recipes. He had a bakery of his own. I mentioned to them that I had thought that baking was considered a job for men, and they both agreed that it was gradually being done by both men and women. Amparo's brother even said that his wife and children had actually taken over his bakery in Quintana Roo.

Amparo is an openly religious person. The rear room of their house serves as a shrine for the Virgin of Fátima, complete with a table decorated as an altar and streamers on the ceiling, although the room itself is cluttered with merchandise. There are hooks for hammocks in the room too, as it doubles as a "guest room." Amparo seems close to the priest, and embroidered one of the altar cloths at the church. She is very Catholic, religious in her speech and in her attitude toward things. She appears to be less related to the old Mayan ways than her sisters. She and Eduardo were patrons of the first *gremio,* the procession of the Agricultural Guild during the Fiesta of san Diego. This was a Spanish custom brought over in the sixteenth century, and while it has disappeared from most other parts of Mexico, it is celebrated in Chan Kom much as it was when the Spanish introduced it.

For eight days before the Feast of San Diego, various families take turns making candles. They make four decorated candles that look like the moon and the stars, with inserts of colored shiny paper, and four smaller candles which go in front. The holders for them are passed from family to family, and different people own different molds. Any family can volunteer to make the candles; it is not restricted to the Guild, the *agricultores,* as it was originally. Marta's husband is one of the candle makers. He and another man made the candles this year for Amparo and Eduardo. Just at sunset people carrying banners are led by the marching band over to the house where the candles are being offered. When the procession of people arrives at the house with the candles, the family comes out, and there is another procession to the church. Evening mass is held. The next morning at six the procession begins again, band music, fireworks and all. The bells ring, and there is another mass. The first banner I saw leading the procession read *"Gremio de los Agricultores de Chan Kom 1954."* The first night, Felicia, her sisters, and her brothers marched behind their parents carrying the ritual candles and the great banners through the plaza and to the church, looking so serious and proud. After seeing the whole celebration, I understood why the women had explained *gremio* as a generic term to apply to everything that accompanies the offering— fireworks, band music, and the procession, instead of defining it in its true form, which is simply "guild."

Felicia and her sisters were very excited when the November Fiesta started. Their city cousins came from Mérida to stay with them for the week, sleeping in the guest room with Fátima. The room was filled with hammocks and giggling girls. It really resembled an old-fashioned slumber party, with the girls all fussing over each other's hair, experimenting with make-up, chattering a mile a minute. The night of the dance, Felicia, the younger sisters, and guests all followed Amparo across the street to the benches set aside in front of the town hall, all in *huipiles,* with rose-colored ribbons and bows in their hair. Mothers and aunts came and sat with their young girls, while the men milled around outside, fortifying themselves with beer, gradually getting up the courage to come in and ask for a dance.

When I went to their house to say goodbye in November, Eduardo and Amparo were sitting together at the tortilla table having a snack. They looked happy and peaceful. We began to talk about dreams, and Eduardo said that he often had a dream in which he was driving a car. "It's not always the same color, and I don't know what kind of car it was. I always wake up just before I crash. . . Do you think I can learn to drive?" He asked if people outside of Chan Kom were brighter than those of the village. Was it hard to drive a car? I offered to give him a lesson, and we set a time for later. But when I came back for him he had since decided not to try it.

Amparo had things she wanted to talk about.

> May I ask you a question that I've been worrying about? How can I lose weight? I'm getting heavier and heavier. My daughter Adelina likes to be thin (she looks plump to me). She eats only eggs and milk and fruit and only a few tortillas and not much bread.

She added that she was very tired and that baking bread made her back ache. I gave her the name of the doctor I knew when she asked about not having any more children. She wondered why the pain in her back never went away. She has a regular doctor in Valladolid, and it seemed strange to me that he had neither suggested anything to her about how she might lose weight, nor done anything about the pain in her back.

On my last visit to Chan Kom, Amparo and felicia met me at the front of their store, happy to see me again and eager to talk. I had brought with me an article from *Diario de Yucatan,* 27th of February, showing the *actos* of the road opening. Felicia and her sisters all began talking at once about what was happening in Chan Kom. The younger girls had gone to see the *sacbé* already, but Felicia had had to keep store and so had not been able to try out the new road. I suggested that she drive out with Victoria and me (and a few others who just had to go again) to see the *sacbé,* and on to Xanla to see the Mayan ruins where they had just discovered a tomb full of treasures. However, during the night after the discovery someone had gone in and stolen all the gold and other treasures. As we stopped to look at the tomb, women and children from Xanla came out to greet us. Their homes were very close to the ruin, yet when we asked them about what had happened there they seemed completely ignorant of the whole incident. It was a nice afternoon, and I was glad that Felicia had been able to get away from "her" store, as the people in the village refer to it, for a little fun and excitement.

ANITA

On my first day in Chan Kom, after Don Trini had invited me to stay in the front room of his house, he asked me if I had brought my hammock with me. As I had not been intending to stay, I had not, and a young girl of about thirteen came over and started insisting that I buy a hammock from her. Don Trini had offered to let me use one of his, so I declined her offer, but she was very persistent. This bothered me, as I did not want to get into a buying relationship with people before I got to know them. But every time I would walk by her house, Rosita, the girl, or her mother, Doña Anita, would call out if I wished to buy a hammock or some embroidery. I did not wish to approach them in that way, so I did not really get a chance to have a conversation with Anita until my second visit to Chan Kom.

My first impression of Anita, naturally, was that she was somewhat aggressive. Also, her children seemed to be less well cared for than the others I saw. Her baby girl always wore a ragged fancy dress and nothing else. Her children went around with runny noses, and were not as clean as the other children. Part of this impression, though, had come from what the other women told me about Anita. There is some underlying antagonism between Anita and the rest of the Mecab family, Anita being married to Don Demetrio, or Talo, who is a son of Don Trini by his first wife, Hilaria. The problem is never talked about, but they obviously do not associate with her, she herself has no relatives in Chan Kom. Doña Victoria, who told me frankly that she dislikes her, told me that Anita beats her children regularly, although she admitted that she never saw her doing it. The houses of Don Trini and Demetrio are so close that it is almost impossible not to hear what is happening in one when you are in the other. At night, when Anita's youngest child cries as she is put to bed, Doña Luz says, "Ah, Dona Anita is beating Elena again." I asked her how she knew Elena was being beaten, but all they would say was that Anita is *"muy delicada"* (very touchy).

After several attempts, I found that the only place I could really talk with Anita was inside her own house. Her kitchen is very comfortable, fresh and open. She has all her things placed conveniently around her—not orderly, but very homey. As I got to know her better, it seemed to me that this was a reflection of her attitude toward many things, that she was simply easy going, and wanted her children to feel free and happy. She would let them run around dirty rather than make them keep clean all the time, and she liked them to dress as they pleased. She is herself as unselfconscious as her children—exuberant, talkative, and much less reserved than the other women. (Ana, for example, was embarrassed when I came to visit her and her hair was not put up, and Victoria was upset that I took a picture of her when she was barefoot.) Also, I have never seen Anita use the white powder that the other women put on, especially when they dress up in city clothes, and I have never seen her dressed in anything but a *huipil,* In repose, Anita does not seem very distinctive, but when she is singing or talking she becomes vivacious and quite attractive. She has a spontaneous laugh, and as Bill Herman, a student who visited Chan Kom, said, "She seems quite happy, quite open and sexy." She was the only one of the women who invited him in to talk with her and her husband, and who did not seem to be embarrassed by his presence.

The only person Anita talked about much was her dead mother-in-law, Doña Hilaria. They had been quite close. She told me that she and Demetrio had moved out of the compound when Hilaria had died, and I thought that perhaps there had been some tension with Doña Luz, Don Trini's second (unmarried) wife, as she assumed Hilaria's full position. But perhaps the trouble simply came from the crowded situation; four families and their children had been living together in that compound, and it is easy to see how they might have gotten on each other's nerves. Nevertheless, Hilaria and Anita were quite close, and she tells me that her daughter Elena looks just like Hilaria.

Anita has a wonderful relationship with all of her children. She is very relaxed and playful with them. They all know games and songs, even the youngest, and they enjoy playing and singing with their mother. Rosita, thirteen, is the eldest, and has an unusually close relationship with her mother; the other children are Emiliano, eight, Esperanza, six, Fermin, four, and Elena, one and a half. Emiliano became one of my favorite children on my last trip. He is very bright and artistic, and is always modeling things out of clay. He was good at doing pigs and squirrels, and as a farewell gift, made me a candle holder which he baked in the sun until it was hard. Rosita runs most of the Village errands for her mother: hauling water, taking the corn to be ground in the *molino,* shopping. In part, Rosita is simply being helpful, but I think this lack of contact on Anita's part with the rest of the women goes back to the old problem. Another important indication that there is friction between the families is seen in the fact that although Demetrio is quite fair, and Anita's children are the lightest skinned of all the children in Chan Kom, Don Trini never speaks of the children or comments on their beauty and skin color. This is unusual for him as he is quick to praise his other grandchildren.

During one conversation Anita told me a good deal about her childhood and early marriage to Demetrio. She says that she is religious because her mother was *"muy catolica,"* and taught all her daughters to go to mass and say their prayers. She said:

> Ever since I was little, I was taught to sing the rosary. I have lots of books here, and now my girl Rosita is learning to read. . . . My poor mother was forty-five when she died. We were young when she died. She left us her books. When we were older, my father said, 'Your poor mother knew how to read and write, and you're going to learn those things too.' And we all learned how to do those things. And these copies that I have here were my mother's. It's her handwriting, but I copied it. We all copied it.

She told me that she learned how to read well because the town where she was born, Muchucux-cah was very far away and the teachers would come and stay a long time because it was so difficult to get there.

She said she thought that it was good they had learned all of those things. Demetrio must have felt the same way. When I asked him how he happened to fall in love with Anita, he told me that it was because she knew how to read well, was hard working, and knew a little Spanish. Anita is Demetrio's second wife. Don Trini had forced him to marry his first cousin; all of their children had died except for one girl, a cripple, who is a *nana* in the house of his sister. Some of the other men in the village told me that she was lazy, and did not want to work as hard as Trio did, so one day she took her little girl and left. She wanted him to go to court with her for a formal divorce, but he would not go. He had been told that she was planning to slander him, and there would be nothing he could do about it.

Anita was fourteen when Demetrio asked her parents for permission to marry her. He was thirty-two. I asked her what her feelings about marrying a man so much older than she had been, and if she had not been in love with one of the young boys in Muchuca Cah. "Yes, there were young boys there, but no—I thought, this isn't my luck, and I didn't fall in love." Her family had been impressed by Demetrio, and he had agreed to pay for her food for three years, until she was seventeen and old enough to marry. The traditional gifts of breads and chocolate were made, but not by Don Trini, who was angry that Demetrio and his wife had separated and so refused to have anything to do with it. Instead they were given by Demetrio's brother, Alvaro, because "he wanted his brother to be happy," and everyone was satisfied. They have been married for fourteen years now, and they say they are very happy with one another. When Rosita had been born, however, they had not been as well off, and the baby had been very sick.

> We were very poor when Rosita was born. She had few clothes, and those were given to her by Demetrio's poor mother. And when Rosita was born, she cried at first for almost three days in a row. She cried and cried and cried. We went to the *h-men*—my grandfather was the *h-man* and knew how to cure people. Rosita was crying and crying, so my husband went to my grandfather and brought him here. And he said, 'the earth where she was born is not good. You have to change it. If you want to cure her, you must take her to the place where you were born.' And so we took her to Muchuca Cah, to my old house. She never got any sleep. I got sick too, and I thought she would never get well. But when we took her to Muchuca Cah, my grandfather said that she wouldn't die, that she'd begin to grow. So we killed two *gallinas* and had the ceremony, and afterwards we went to the meal and brought a candle. And when this was over and night came, I held Rosita and began to pray to Our Savior that we would be able to sleep. Afterwards, we fell asleep. And she slept so well! The first night! I was very satisfied. So now when I forget to pray, the baby has to cry. (She laughs.) And she grew and grew. Then her little brother was born. But he died, and my grandfather said that it was because we didn't do the same ceremony for him. But Rosita is still growing, and I don't think she is going to die.

I asked her what kind of ceremony she did when Emiliano was born, as he was the next in line.

> I didn't do anything, you know, because Rosita has this double crown in the back of her head. Ha. And it was because of this that her little brother didn't grow, and then he died. And so when Emiliano was born, my grandfather said, 'If you want your children to grow, if you want them to live, when you first are bathing them, first cook an egg and hold it over the double-crown. Then they will live.' And I did this and Emiliano didn't die and is growing. . . .

When Emiliano was born, Anita and Demetrio were living on a ranch up in their *milpa*. They were poor, and it was easier for them to work there together. They stayed there for ten years, and both remember the time as the happiest in their lives.

> ANITA: When I began to work with him in the *milpa*, I sowed, I chopped, I harvested. Everything . . . we're thinking of making another visit there. We want to spend two or three years there. The school where the children go is close, about two kilometers, so they will keep on going. I want to raise my *gallinas* there . . . we want to repeat the year.

> DEMETRIO: We were happy there. At the ranch we didn't have as many expenses as we do here in Chan Kom.

> ANITA: At the ranch we almost never wasted money on things as we do here, for chocolate and coca-cola.

> DEMETRIO: At the ranch there aren't those things. If we came into town once or twice a week, that was enough. There was game up there, and I would go out with my gun for birds to eat . . . We had *gallinas, pavos, cochinas* . . . everything. We had cows that give milk. It is very pretty there.

I know that Anita loves the *milpa* because when Demetrio is gone on a trip (he is a traveling salesman) she and her children go to work up there. She walks with great energy, and they follow her like little chickens in a flock, very noisy and happy. But according to Jorge, Demetrio's reason for wanting to return to the ranch is purely economic. In addition to being a salesman and having a *milpa*, Demetrio also is a buyer for his brother Eduardo, and has a share of cattle in the *socio* (cooperative farm). This is another problem in itself, and may have something to do with the bad feelings between the Macabs and his family. Demetrio is in bad repute with his brothers because he has not been paying his share of the costs for taking care of the cattle. He has thirty head of cattle, compared to Jorge's six head and Don Trini's fifteen, but Jorge says that he is not paying him to feed the cattle and take care of them. He is *muy duro* (hard to get along with), his brothers feel, and *codo* (stingy). It seems especially bad to them that he is cheating his own family.

Demetrio, of course, said nothing of this to me, and things seemed fine between him and Alvaro and Jorge when they came to his house for Anita's saint day. She was thirty years old, and I brought her a can of sweet-smelling insect repellent to ward off the bugs in the *milpa*. The party was for dinner. The chicken had been offered to Anita's saint, and when I got there she insisted that I sit at the table with Demetrio. I sat down, thinking she would join us since it was not a large gathering, but then Jorge and Alvaro came in (without their wives), and she still sat there, making tortillas at her own party. So I said, "This isn't right—it's your party. Let Rosita make the tortillas and you come eat at the table." But she said "No, we'll eat ours later." I went to sit down with her, but she was embarrassed so I returned to the table. This was somewhat surprising because I had found that when families are not in a large compound together, like that of Don Trini, the men and women usually sit together at the table. After dinner I asked Anita to sing for us. Her voice is lovely, and when I returned to the house of Don Trini, I played the tape I had made of her, so they could hear. Jorge asked me to play it again so that Antonio could hear. It seemed that they had never heard her sing before. After it was over, Doña Luz began to speak, but Jorge had noticed that I had switched the machine to record and he said to her, "Don't say anything, the tape is on." And they began speaking in Mayan.

The day before, when I had been learning about the different jobs Demetrio did, Anita told me that she used to have a sewing machine and had made excellent embroidery. But Demetrio thought there would be conflicts between taking care of the children and sewing.

> Demetrio doesn't like it. When I was pregnant, I left my sewing machine. Doña Victoria bought it. Because it isn't good to work like that when you're pregnant. I was doing embroidery, like Doña Victoria does, and when Demetrio would go on a trip, he would take it with him to sell, and then he would bring me the money. But when I was sick with child I couldn't do it anymore. When the child was born, it was the same, until it was six month old, or more. Demetrio told me it would be better to sell the machine, because with all these children, you can't work with the machine. Not like Doña Victoria because she doesn't have children to care for. Ha. She does very good work, like a man. She doesn't know what it's like to have a child.

I told her that Victoria had a little girl who had died.

> Only one. Ha. She hasn't had a lot of children, and because of this she can work very well. She's hardly ever sick—only fever or *catarrah* and these go away in two or three days and she can go back to work with her machine. But us—no. We can't. And so I sold my machine, and that machine was what I wanted since I was a little girl. I liked it very much. Ha. And I liked to live doing that in my house. . . .

I asked her why Demetrio did not sell a few of his cattle and buy the machine back.

> He has to finish the house first—put bricks down instead of a dirt floor. And he's going to fix it all up. And when it is done the way he wants it, he'll buy my machine. Ha. We will buy it for Rosita, and teach her how to embroider.

I recalled an earlier conversation I had with Anita when we were also talking about children. I asked her if she wanted any more; she had said no, she would give anything not to have more children, so that she could work and take care of the ones she had. But when I asked the same question when Demetrio was there, she said nothing and he said, "Who knows how many children we will have?" Later, Anita said to me,

> All my married life I have only had one period between my children. Now I have a period. Is there really a way that women can keep from having more children and live with their husbands? I've always wondered how Ana and Jorge have managed to have only one child. I've wanted to ask Ana, but I had *verguenza*.

At that time I told Anita about the Mayan-speaking doctor who had just returned from attending a special IUD conference in Mexico City. I told her something about the various forms of birth control, and said I hoped that she and Demetrio could go to the clinic in Xochenpich to see the doctor there. She seemed amazed that there were so many different methods of control, and I hoped that she could convince Demetrio to take her there.

The conversation turned to Rosita. I told Anita I had read in a book that many Mayan mothers do not tell their daughters about menstruation before their first period. And then the girls do not know what is happening and they are afraid. She told me that it had happened to Rosita.

> I didn't tell her. She was about twelve when she had her first period, and she cried and said, 'What am I going to do? What's happening to me?' (She laughs.) I asked her what the matter was and she said her clothes were blood stained. So I told her that's what happens to a woman, and that before she could go around with the boys but now she couldn't. Now she had become a woman, and I told her, the little girls don't know about these things, but you know and now you are a woman, now you are our age. They say it's a sin to tell girls anything about periods before they have them.

I asked her if in all those years Rosita had not seen that she had bloodstains on her clothes sometimes.

> No. Before no. You wash your clothes during your period apart from the other clothes. But before Rosita's period she was talking about it with her cousins and asked me if it wasn't so, and I said no, it's not so, because it hadn't happened to her yet. But now it's time for her to start going to dances. And I told her, now you may begin to dance, but you mustn't think that just because you can do this that you can go talk with the boys. But if at the dance they talk to you about marriage, it isn't good to answer them

there. If anyone mentions marriage to you, tell him to come to me or your father. Her father hasn't talked to you about these things—only I do. I tell her about all these things. She sees them, and knows if they are good or bad.

I told her I thought that was important, because the life of a woman could be very dangerous.

Yes, that's true. And this thing that happens to us every month—it isn't good to get wet at that time. We bathe, but with hot water, nothing cold. And nothing cold to drink. This thing of taking care of ourselves, I think it's the ideas of our grandmothers. And because of this, we go on growing and getting larger, my father says. When it is your time, you don't eat oranges, you don't allow yourself to get wet, you don't eat lemon, you don't wash your hair. All those things we can't do.

Later, when Demetrio came in, I asked again about Rosita. I asked if she were big enough to go with boys.

BOTH: No.

ELMENDORF: But she seems so big and pretty!

ANITA: But she still doesn't know how to dance. She will learn at this party, and I will prepare her clothes for her.

ELMENDORF: And what kind of preparation are you giving her? To tell her how to behave with boys—does she know?

(This is misinterpreted.)

BOTH: No.

ELMENDORF: Do fathers talk with their daughters about sex life? (No one speaks.) No?

DEMETRIO: (Shortly.) No.

ELMENDORF: You don't tell her about the precautions she should take? (They talk briefly in Mayan, more relaxed.)

ANITA: Oh, the precautions. I do, but not her father. When we are alone I tell her the things she shouldn't do and that she shouldn't go with a man. Ha. This is what I explain to her.

I had talked earlier with Anita about what they told their children about sexual matters, but I had wanted Demetrio's reaction too. I didn't think that they told their children directly, but it seemed impossible for a child not to learn something about it, living together in such close quarters. I had asked Anita where she and her husband had their sexual life—in the room with the children, or in another room.

ANITA: We sleep here with the children.

ELMENDORF: And they don't know what you're doing?

ANITA: Never. When they go to sleep, they go to sleep. (She laughs.) They never know.

ELMENDORF: Not even Rosita?

ANITA: Not even Rosita.

ELMENDORF: And you haven't spoken to her about this?

ANITA: No.

ELMENDORF: Shouldn't you?

ANITA' No—it's a sin.

ELMENDORF: Won't she be surprised by a man sometime? . . . and she won't know what's happening. Or when she marries?

ANITA: (Laughs.) Well, when you marry it is very surprising because you don't know.

ELMENDORF: But perhaps the children would have learned from the animals. You live very closely with them.

ANITA: I don't think they pay any attention to it. They don't understand.

ELMENDORF: And about how many times do a Mayan man and woman have intercourse?

ANITA: (Scolds a child in background, hesitating.) Only from time to time. Because my husband—that is my custom—he rarely stays here, my husband with me. That's the way it is. The others—I think those here, because their husbands are here all their life, I think that—almost all week. (She laughs.) Every night. But for me, my husband is a traveling salesman and so he hardly ever stays here. All his life is like that. He never stays here.

ELMENDORF: But when he comes back, you are very loving?

Anita: (she laughs.) This—yes. When he stays here—yes—because, well, he says, 'I look for other women when I am on the road'—he says—'but I don't want to waste all of my money because I want to leave it to my children.'

And I thought that, if Jorge was right, here was Demetrio's "stinginess" again, manifesting itself in a strange way. Also, it seemed that perhaps here was another possible reason for the antagonism between Anita and the Mecabs—fear that the other men would consider her unattached while Demetrio was away—a situation which her warm, open nature might seem to encourage.

On my field trip to the village in November, I passed Anita sitting on a log stool talking with her children as she and Rosita wove a lovely green and yellow hammock together. Anita would pass the shuttle through to Rosita and Rosita would pass it back to her. All the children were sitting around them on their little log stools, and I wanted to photograph the scene. But the hammock had been finished when I came back with the camera.

Soon after this I saw Doña Anita talking animatedly with Doña Victoria as she helped her thread the sewing machine, the same machine which had once been hers and which she wants back. Her children were out in front playing on the new sidewalk, exploring the newly tiled floors and splashing in the paint. Almost all the houses were being painted—wild mixtures of greens, reds, pinks and yellows. On November 1, the night of the dead, the men painted all through the night, looking very strange with their brushes in the moonlight.

One day when I was returning from lunch, I found that Elena had one eye swollen shut, and her whole face was an angry red. "She put her hand into a bag of lime and threw it over her face and into her mouth," said Anita. "I rinsed it well with honey and water—it should be alright." But early Sunday morning she came and asked if I had any drops for Elena's eye, because it was still closed and badly swollen. I brought the drops, but when I saw her eye I did not think they would be of much use, and suggested that we take her to the doctor. Demetrio was out shopping in Valladolid, so Anita and I piled all her children in the car except for Rosita and Esperanza, who were left to watch the house, and set off for the clinic, on the way there, Anita told me,

> Señora Maria, I am three months pregnant. My last period was when you were here. Ha. I wish I could have gone with you to the clinic then. I feel so awful—even worse than with the others because I don't want another child. I wanted to take care of these I have. I wanted to get a sewing machine and teach Rosita. Ha.

When we got to the clinic, we found that the doctor I knew was not there. The other doctor gave us a wash for Elena's eye, but knowing that he did not approve of my friend's birth control work, I did not talk to him about Anita. He and Anita talked in Mayan together for some time; on the way home she told me that she felt nauseated and dizzy every morning, and I regretted that we had not talked to the doctor about her anyway. At least she got a chance to see where the clinic is, and now with the new road it is possible for her to get there on her own if she needs to.

One afternoon Anita invited me to go with her and Rosita to the house of Don Remijio Hau Mecab, where she had been invited to do the *rezos* for the soul of his dead wife. We were welcomed by his second wife, a small, dignified woman, who invited us into the house. The altar was prepared with four simple candlesticks made from some kind of black metal. They were beautiful. Gourds with *atole* were on the table, and corn bread filled with chicken and pork which had been baked in the earth oven were piled in the center of the altar in front of St. Fatima. The image was covered with plastic and tied around with a string. When I asked why it was covered, they said for no reason, simply to keep it clean. And they asked if they should uncover her and put her dress on for the photograph. I told them yes and a fancy, flimsy dress with cut-outs for her hands was put on the saint.

The house where this was held was of the original Mayan elliptical design, and was placed on a rocky hilltop so that one had the feeling of being on a mountain or up a tree. I could look out through the wooden poles of the house at the children playing in the yard. Rudolfo was playing with little Elena, and the older children had formed a circle in the dirt road and were practicing the *jarana*. Several of the mothers inside kept suggesting that I take pictures of the children instead of the prayer ceremony.

When we arrived, we found two chairs arranged with kneeling pads made of henequen sacks on the dirt floor. A narrow bench was placed just behind the chairs. The room was filled with women and children, and Anita and Rosita began to conduct the ceremony. They initiated all the prayers, the responsive readings, and the singing. When I asked Anita if she were paid to do this, she said no, that it was a great honor to be asked to lead the service, and that several people had requested that she and Rosita come lead the prayers in their house.

(It was interesting to me that the husband for whose wife the *rezos* were made was not present, and that he came in directly after the last prayers were said. These prayers were previously led by the *maestro cantor.*

On the night of the dance, Demetrio was very gracious as I introduced him to some visitors from Chichen Itza. As we talked about the movie I was trying to take, he said that a French film company had done a similar thing several years ago, and that he had arranged a *Cha-Chaac* (a *milpa* ceremony) for them, and that he would be happy to do the same for me so that I could film it next summer. I had not asked him for this, and it seemed to me to show a new kind of trust and confidence in Demetrio's attitude toward me.

Anita's father arrived at the fiesta just as I was leaving Chan Kom. He is tall, slim, and walks with great dignity. Anita wanted me to take his picture, but he was seemingly unaccustomed to foreigners, and very tense. When I told him to move around, as it was a moving picture we were taking, he seemed quite frightened. But we did not spoil his meeting with Anita, and she was busy introducing several other relatives, very cheerful and delighted that they had come for the Fiesta.

As always, it was hard to leave. Maybe I could have understood Anita better if I could have stayed to talk with her family, but then, there is no end to understanding.

FLORA

The younger sister of Victoria and Amparo, is physically quite different from her sisters. She is taller than they are, very buxom, with a
round face which brightens when she smiles. Her shoulder-length hair
is loose, not pulled back in the style of the other women, and she wears
a tight low-cut dress rather than a *huipil.*

Flora was married to Antonio, another son of Don Trini, in a group
ceremony which was performed by a priest several years after they
started living together. (Don Trini and Dona Luz were married in the
same ceremony.) Antonio's choice of Flora was strongly disapproved
by Don Trini, who said that he wanted some new blood in his family.
Don Trini had already decided on a wife for Antonio, so they quarreled. "My father chose another," he told me, "but I didn't like her.
She lived very far away. I hardly knew her. I chose Flora and we started
living together." Eventually Don Trini became reconciled to the situation. When Flora became pregnant with her first child, she and Antonio moved in with Don Trini, sleeping in the masonry building next
to the thatched hut.

Now they have six children. Flora's two eldest sons, Juan and José,
have been "regalado" (literally: made presents of) to Flora's sister
Victoria and her husband Alvaro. They have no children of their own
and have promised to raise the boys like their own sons. The boys are
worked very hard there, however, and lately Juan had been spending
more and more time with his original family. Although Victoria has a
short temper and treats the boys harshly some times, she makes sure
they go to school and even takes an interest in their homework. In this
respect they are better off than their sisters, since Flora takes little
interest in their education, preferring to keep them around the house
to watch over the youngest boys. Alexandria had charge of Andres, and
Eva watched over Martin. They are like little mothers to them. I was
curious as to why Flora took so little interest in her daughters' education, especially since her sisters were both eager for their children or
adopted children to learn. One day she told me:

> When I was little I had *granisos* (sores) all over my body. I was very sick
> and couldn't go to school. When I was well again I was already twelve
> years old and couldn't go anymore. Alexandria will be twelve soon and
> then her first menstrual period will begin. Then she has to stop going to
> school.

I asked why twelve years old was the age when they had to stop. "It's
the custom," she said. But I was worried because I knew that Alexandria could hardly write her name, so I asked whether since the new

young school teachers had come, perhaps Alexandria could keep going a little longer, at least until she could read and write a little. "No, Senora, her *reglas* (periods) will start soon and she'll have to stop. It's the way. She musn't go to school with boys. Antonio will have to teach her." I wondered if he would. Even though he is a former president of the PTA, he showed little interest in the education of his daughters. It also seemed that if he didn't even trouble to make sure that they attended school, it was not likely that he would bother to educate his daughters himself. This is all very unfortunate, because their children really do seem to be behind the others. When I gave crayons and paper to the children to draw with, they could barely sign their names to the pictures, which seemed more like those drawn by pre-school children.

Flora seems to be set apart from the other women. It is not simply that she received almost no education; neither did Victoria or Amparo, and they are eager to learn. Part of it may be extreme shyness. It was always difficult for me to understand her. She is very quiet, although sometimes when talking with other women or playing with her children she would burst into spontaneous laughter. She is tender and loving with her two smallest children, but brusque and demanding with the older ones. She said that she wears a dress rather than a *huipil* "Because Antonio wants me to." Her daughter Alexandria does not have a *huipil* either, and her clothes are always patched and ragged looking. That was another difference. While the other women took great care that their *huipiles* stayed fresh and white, Flora's family seemed to dress in grey rags in comparison. Old clothes for patches were kept in a box in the thatched hut, or in a chest of drawers in the masonry house. This chest is the only piece of furniture in the room besides the home altar, which doubled as a table. Often I would see Flora sewing patches onto their old clothes while they were still wet from being washed, always in a hurried fashion never appearing to take any more time than necessary.

Even though Alexandria has no *huipil* of her own, since she is almost twelve years old she has been taught the art of *huipil* making. It took her eight days to make her first one, done in a simple cross-stitch design with magenta thread. She sold it to Doña Luz. "I gave her nine eggs for it," Luz told me, "and they all hatched! She sold two chickens in Valladolid for twenty-two pesos. She ate one and the rest are still here. She made lots of money which she's saving." Victoria seems to like Zaza, as they sometimes call her, and is eager to teach her how to sew on a sewing machine. She even talked of buying another machine for her to make the teaching easier. Victoria is often concerned about her little sister's family, and I believe she has often given them clothes and even money, such as for the time she wanted Flora to be able to visit their father at his new rancheria. Victoria, as so often is the case, took care of Flora, really raised her as a mother would while they were growing up. She is planning to leave all her property to their two "adopted" sons, whom she really hopes to adopt legally if Flora and Antonio will agree.

Flora does much of the hard work which only the men do in other families. According to Redfield and other ethnographers, as well as word of mouth in the village, carrying the heavy wood is supposed to be done by the men. I never saw Antonio doing this, however. Sometimes Juan would help, and he and his mother would go off together to the forest. One morning I came by to find her out in the yard cutting some wood. "I went to the *monte* with Juan last night and cut the *palso* (long straight poles). Juan carried them back and built the wall." The wall to the thatched hut had been in disrepair, and the new poles made it look much better. Flora was also rebuilding the sideboard, and she paid Juan a peso to help her do some of the more difficult chopping of the logs. She is the only woman with a husband I have ever seen doing work of this kind, and I asked her why Antonio did not help her. "He is too busy with his job," she said. "And too tired when he comes home." Nonetheless, when I asked her whose job was harder, a man's or a woman's, she told me that men had a harder life. "They have to earn money. After washing I can sit in the hammock and sew." But it was rare that I would see Flora quietly sewing or playing with a child. Almost always she was busy washing, helping Luz with meals, cleaning up the kitchen, building, or drawing and carrying the average forty pails of water she hauls in a day.

With all her wook and children, I wondered what Flora felt about birth control. When I asked her if she wanted more children or if she would like to stop at six, she said:

> "Oh, the midwife has seen that I won't have any more children. I don't need to go to the doctor, Señora. She is *muy comadrona* (a very good midwife). She could tell when Martin was born that there wouldn't be others. And if women can't have babies, she knows what to do also."

During my November visit, Flora told me, "Martin is going to be baptized Sunday in the morning. I don't know when, but Sunday, when the priest is in town." But the ceremony had to be cancelled at the last moment. Alvaro, as godfather, had gone to Mérida to get the baptismal clothes, but when they were unwrapped Victoria found that the *gorro* (cap) had been left out, and that they would have to wait for another trip to Mérida. When everything was finally ready the second time, I was waiting in Luz's kitchen, thinking to go to the church with Don Trini and Luz. The service was to take place between the *gremio* and the dance. Flora came in with several pieces of paper, and asked Don Trini to read them for her and find which one was Martin's birth certificate. When it was already past time for the ceremony, I asked Don Trini when he was going. "He can't go to church," said Luz with some surprise, "He hasn't even taken a bath!" So I hurried over alone and came in, unfortunately, just at the end of the ceremony. The *padrino* and *madrina* of the *bautismo* were Alvaro and Victoria, who are also godparents to all of the rest of Flora's children. Earlier that week I had seen Ana playing with Martin in the hammock. It was the first time I had seen her being affectionate with any child but Rudolfo, so I told her that she seemed quite fond of him. "Oh yes," she said, "he is my *ahijado,*" meaning that she had been his madrina of the *hetzmek* ceremony, and Jorge had been the padrino.

I felt that one reason it was difficult to get to know Flora was the same reason it was difficult for me to speak alone with Luz. Both Antonio and Don Trini are eager to talk, even garrulous, and any time they were in the room the women would always defer to them. I would ask them a question, and either one of the men would answer, saying something like, "She doesn't have much Spanish and doesn't understand," or one of the women would say, "Ask Don Trini" or "Ask Antonio," This, in addition to the impossibility of getting a moment completely alone with either Luz or Flora, made understanding difficult.

MARTA

One of the first days I was in Chan Kom, while returning from a visit to Doña Pamela, who was making *chuyubs* out in the colonia, Alexandria asked me if I wanted to stop by and see her Aunt Marta, another daughter of Don Trini. We turned into a big garden off the road, two houses behind Eduardo's store. The yard seemed spacious and on the right hand side I saw a great tin tub of water on a slab of stone, warming in the sun. This intrigued me because it seemed such an obvious way to save wood and effort. We called from the entrance of the traditional Mayan hut and a voice answered "Come in." Inside was a very fat woman sitting at a sewing machine facing the sunny courtyard. She greeted us with a smile, "I like my machine looking out because I can see the birds that way, and whatever else is passing." At her feet by the treadle a turkey was setting on her eggs, which Marta said were ready to hatch any day. Alexandria went home to take care of the baby, and as Marta was alone in her house, we were able to have a long, uninterrupted conversation.

My first impressions of Marta were that she was very frank and open, "unattractively attractive." She is said to resemble her mother, Hilaria, more than her sisters, and has very fair skin. To our Northern eyes she wouldn't be called a blonde, but the Mecab's refer to her as the *"rubia."* She has buck teeth, very red gums, and does not have the Mayan look which I have seen in many of the other faces. "She has blood like you Americans," Don Trini would say over and over again.

She had a ready laugh, and as we went through the questions from the Fromm questionnaire, she was open in her answers and free in conversation. One of the first things she told me was that her father had made her get married when she was only thirteen; she had not known the boy and was in tears at the ceremony. She had not even begun menstruation at the time of her marriage, and her husband was only seventeen. She said that Don Trini wanted her to get married because he thought he was going to die. However, sister Gabriela told me later that it was because one of her cousins wanted to marry her, and Don Trini did not want that to happen again. Marta now seems very content, and told me:

> I've never had an unhappy time with my husband. I love him. Women have it easy in their cool thatched huts with their happy fat piglets.

I have never seen her when she was not at ease smiling. Her husband, Rufino, also seems to be very happy. They have a *milpa* and live primarily from their corn crop, which was excellent this year. They proudly showed me some of the ears of corn and had me taste the *atole* they made from it. They make their living from corn and pigs in more of the traditional way than others in the family. They have a well in their back yard, and lead a fairly autonomous life. I did not feel that Marta had much of a desire for gain in material terms the way, for instance, Victoria seemed to.

Rufino is on the town council. I had been pleased at first to meet a new name on the council, only to find out that he was, through Marta, also related to another Mecab. The first time I saw him was in Amparo's kitchen where he was sitting at the table, pasting shiny bits of paper into beeswax, making candles for the first *gremio.* This ceremony is part of the week long festivities for San Diego, patron saint of Chan Kom. A statue of San Diego was found in a cave by Don Trini's father years ago. According to many, San Diego performs miracles for the people of Chan Kom, and they have great faith in him. Marta's daughter was sick during one of my visits, and despite the fact that I had taken her to the clinic for a shot, they all were sure that it was San Diego who had made her well. "When my daughter was sick I went to the church and asked San Diego to make her well. Now she is much better," Marta explained. The only place that was not well, she said, was the place where the shot had been given—and they seemed to blame me and the nurse for the fact that the shot hurt. The credit for the cure went to San Diego.

Marta has three sons and two daughters, both of whom are married. Luisa, the elder, is married to a very dapper one-eyed man from another town. They came back during the fiesta with their two little children. Luisa went with her uncle, Clemente, one of those days, in his truck to Valladolid, leaving her four year old son behind. The boy was having a tantrum on the curb and people were watching and teasing him. I asked why he was crying so and Marta explained. "Every time my daughter leaves she tells her son she will never come back. That is why he is crying." "But why does she do that?" I asked. Marta did not know. "Perhaps to make him strong." She added later that when his mother came back she whipped the boy for making a scene. "That is her way. She says she is going to leave every time a car comes to town so he will do it." This did not disturb Marta; she just laughed. Jorge, everybody's favorite uncle, began to comfort the boy, but when the boy threw sand at him he soon was laughing at him too.

Marta's sons, like Anita's, seem interested in learning and were always asking the meanings of words, remembering, repeating. I noticed one time that Marta's boys had on sandals while Anita's wore the hot, plastic shoes worn by the men for fiestas, which Jorge and Antonio wear even when they walk into town. They are made to look like leather but are made of cheap plastic and strings. Some of the people seem to think that shoes, even plastic ones, are a sign of "*categoria*," that they put one higher up in the world than wearing *huaraches*. This parallels the feeling that the dress is better than the *huipil*. Marta and Rufino do not seem to be caught in these feelings, and their children are on the whole very secure and happy—cared about but not controlled.

During one of my visits the children had gone fifteen leagues to spend the *semana santa* (holy week) with relatives in Ixmuka. Leonor had gone to sell pigs, and Angel, age sixteen, to play the dumbo drum in *La Banda Tropical*. The two younger boys, Gustavo, thirteen, and Hugo, eleven, are very bright and draw interesting pictures, some of which look like part of their mother's embroidery. Their godfather is the doctor in Valledolid, an unusual choice in Chan Kom. (The two daughters, however, are godchildren of Don Trini.)

Marta and Rufino recently bought a house on the corner of the plaza, just across from Marta's brother Eduardo. During the fiesta they fixed up the front room as a store and had a wooden table with benches and candles outside. They served coffee and *atole,* and were thinking that if there was enough trade, they would keep the shop there permanently. I watched the fiesta from there the first night. Leonor was there too, with her six-year-old daughter. They had her dressed for the fiesta, with her hair up like the other women's and wearing long elegant earrings. I couldn't help laughing, watching her primp, especially as she began to powder—she powdered the whole room! Later on in the evening, Marta started talking about dances and told me, "If women dance the new dances they get pregnant. *Como dice mi pobre mamá,* (as my poor mother used to say) women are like *calabazas,* (squash, i.e., with many seeds) with a little bit of carelessness, ha, you have a child."

BERTA

During my last visit to Chan Kom, I talked at length with Juan Pituh, the *Registro Civil.* His office was right next to Victoria's house, where I was staying, and I was interested in the various records of vital statistics which he kept on the village. When I explained to him that I was primarily interested in understanding the role of women in Chan Kom, he said proudly, "You must meet my wife, Berta. She is the treasurer, and the first woman to serve on the town council of Chan Kom."

I walked out to their house, down the road by the church, through the mud where the pigs were lazily enjoying themselves and across the stepping stones to the masonry building. I thought that it must have been hard on Juan Pituh to move away from his family's large house on the plaza. His family was one of the original families in Chan Kom. They had come before the Mecabs, but when the Protestants were forced out of town, the Pituhs lost most of their property, which included the corner house with its lovely second floor and the room with the balcony facing the square where I was staying. (It now belongs to Alvaro and Victoria.) Juan is one of the few Pituhs left in Chan Kom, and the only property he has kept is the small office building on the plaza, his present house, his *parcela* (lot) of *ejido* land, and a vacant lot just off the plaza where his sons are constructing a masonry house when and as they have the time and the money. Their son Jaime later told me, "When we don't have a job—and there aren't many ways to earn money here—we work together building the house." To be able to do masonry work is a skill admired by many villagers who know only how to build the *jacal* (thatched hut).

I felt a difference immediately as I entered their home. It seemed not Mayan, although both Juan and Berta were Mayan, and as though it did not belong in Chan Kom. I had a feeling of urban poverty, of the barrios of Mexico City. What was different? The furniture, for one thing. There were no rough benches of hand-hewn wood, and no folding chairs or low wooden stools of log like everyone else used. There were high tables and chairs which turned out to be very comfortable, but the whole arrangement was different from the other houses I had seen. There were no hammocks, no home altar or Mayan cross. The walls were decorated with calendars, framed wedding pictures, and a large map which one of the children had made in school. We walked through the long dark house out into the kitchen where I had been invited for refreshments. It was the only kitchen I saw in Chan Kom which was set up in the masonry building rather than in a thatched hut out back. There was a cement floor rather than the swept earth of the other kitchens, torn oil cloth on the sideboards rather than the scrubbed mahogany, and there was a tall spindlylegged table in the middle of the room. Berta served lemonade in glasses, not *jicaras,* (gourds) and poured from a pitcher. There was an embroidered cloth on the table. I wondered why this family was so different, and if it was this difference that set Berta so completely apart from the other women.

I tried to understand why my first impression of her was such a negative one. She seemed somehow lacking in the natural beauty of the other women I had come to know. Perhaps it was the dress I always saw her in—bright pink, stretched at the seams, with dark perspiration rings under the arms. It had none of the easy grace, the comfortableness and simple beauty of the *huipiles.* But it was more than that. Physically she bore a great resemblance to her brother Abel, and neither of them had the oriental Mayan face of the others. It was narrow and pointed of chin, tense, marked with worry lines. There was something about Berta I did not trust, but I tried very hard to overcome that feeling. I had initially reacted the same way to her husband, with his strangely deep voice and his formal clothes and shoes. (But primarily with him I felt my reaction was caused by his marked divergent squint which made direct eye contact impossible.) I began to understand my reactions and tried to balance them with a more impartial state of mind, but wondered if Berta or the other women were at fault in their separation from one another. There seemed to be no mutual affection between them at all. None of my friends had mentioned her to me, even though she was an obvious person for me to talk to since she was the only woman member on the Town Council. Perhaps some of the resentments from the Catholic-Protestant feud still lingered, even though Berta is a Mecab.

After the lemonade, we moved back into the living room. All the chairs had been pulled up and the children crowded around, listening, but all the while busily making *margaritas* (daisies) from henequen fibre. Even the four-year-old was using a large needle and seemed to be completely engrossed in winding the thread around the points on the little frame. He even threaded the needle for himself as I watched with surprise and admiration. To have more privacy with Berta, I asked if the children could leave the room for a while, even though they were very quiet and well-behaved. The second to the oldest son, Jaime, stayed behind. The eldest son, a seventeen-year-old named Thomás, was working as a watchman at the road camp, keeping an inventory of the equipment. He would return to school when his job was finished. Jaime is fifteen, and still in the *secondaria,* which he attends in Mérida. Both he and Thomás live there with their grandmother when they go to school. Now he was home to help his father work the *milpa* they own of some one hundred and fifty hectares. He was a handsome boy, neatly dressed, with a voice almost identical to his father's. He seemed self-confident and almost dignified. I asked him what interests he had, what he most wanted to do. "Well, I want to do well in the school, in my studies, on my exams. . . I might like to be an electrician—that would be good." And now with the road coming, what changes did he think it would bring? "Oh, it is going to be much better. Easier to travel." He was very enthusiastic about it and so was Berta. She talked proudly of her brother Lorenzo, who was a federal teacher in Chihuahua, quite a distance away. It would be much easier now for their family to get together during vacation, and it was obvious that would make a big difference in their lives.

Berta's mother lives in Mérida with some of her five children, and with Tomás and Jaime when school is in session. Her husband, Berta's father is Ignacio Mendoza. According to Doña Luz, he is a half-brother to Don Trini, but his *padrino* had him change his name from Mecab to Mendoza. Although now working at one of the cultural missions in

Vera Cruz as a mason, he keeps his home in Mérida. One of his other children living in Chan Kom is Abel, who readopted the surname 'Mecab' and married his cousin, the daughter of Pascual Mecab. He runs the store on the corner and is the current President of the PTA.

Don Juan's parents are dead. One sister lives in Cozumel, an island off the coast of Yucatan, where she has a small store and sells embroidery to tourists. His youngest sister, nineteen-year-old Morena, moved in with them when their parents died. She spends a lot of time visiting with other relatives, especially the sister in Cozumel. She will take the bus with a younger relative, bringing embroidery and the *henequen* daisies the family makes, to sell in Cozumel or wherever else she goes. She is very slim and attractive, and her face brightens when she tells of the freedom she has to do what she wants. She says that she loves being a *soltera* (single) because it gives her time to *"divertirme"*—to enjoy herself as she pleases.

When I asked Jaime what profession he would like to have, I repeated the question to Berta. She said that most of all she would like to be a *modista* (seamstress). Then she would be able to make her own clothes. Also, I think, it was a matter of pride; she wanted her own profession.

Among the first things Berta and I talked about were her memories as a child. She thought of her days in school.

> I remember the school when I was a little girl, studying, weaving, working with the teacher. . . My father was working in the cultural mission with Sr. Villa Rojas. He worked in Vera Cruz for five years in the Papaloapan Project. He was learning little by little. Sr. Alfonso always asked about my father's children, where they lived and how they were. And he began to know about them. This is when I was a little girl. He knew my father by the name of Ignacio Mendoza. . . We were living here when the cultural mission came to Chan Kom. He was teaching then. And Sr. Alfonso became my godfather. . . I have memories of my mother too. She taught us all to work when we were little, to make a little money, to help each other when we were growing up. She helped us. . .

And what did she remember as the time of her life when she was most content?

> Oh, when we are in the house like this, resting, talking, with the children. We sit, we sing a while, we recite, just like we are, here. I like it very much that the children learn, that they try hard in their studies so they can advance.

I was sorry then that I had asked the children to leave, so I apologized to her and asked if she would not like for them to come back in. "Yes, you see, when someone from the outside comes to our home, we feel it is a way for all of us to learn." So the children came back in, eagerly but quietly, and Berta and I went on talking. I asked her about her work in the committee.

> I am the treasurer. I write out the minutes, keep statistics, make *oficios* (official letters). And if my husband is out of town during the day, working on the road as he is now, I am in charge of the Office of the Registro Civil. I have a key.

And later on that week we went together into the small room which serves as the office. It smelled of tropical wood and musty paper. In the back cupboard, in complete disarray, were the books kept chronologically by year on the birth, deaths, marriages, and one small volume on divorces (only three were recorded, the last one in 1940). While we were there a young couple came in to register the birth of their three-week-old son. Berta took the baby's foot and fingerprints, recording everything meticulously in the heavy ledger.

One incident occurred, however, which made me wonder how completely the other men on the council accepted Berta's presence. It was when Don Trini had returned from Mérida, and an argument was going on in his house about who should have the responsibility for planning the governor's breakfast, who would do the cooking, and so on. Don Trini was angry that they had expected Luz to do all the work and him to do all the planning. In the end, the breakfast was held in the house of the son of Don Pascual, next to the Palacio Municipal. Luz, Berta, and many of the other women helped fix the meal. I asked why Berta had not been in on the planning. "That's right. She should have been," they said. But she obviously had been forgotten. And she was not at the table with the governor during the meal, as were all the other members of the Council. Later she told me that she had been helping with the preparations, and that "I told the governor I was the treasurer of the *Junta de Autoridades* when he came out to thank the women, and he congratulated me!"

I asked her if she wasn't afraid to be the only woman on the committee since they had to go into Mérida for the meetings. I wondered if her husband let her go alone. "No, I'm not afraid. When we have to go to Mérida, I go with one of my sons, Tomás or Jaime. We stay with my family there." And her face lit up as she described the trips. I thought that seeing her family must play a large part of her enjoyment of the official visits.

From the Erich Fromm questionnaire, I asked Berta to define love in her own words. She was thoughtful. "It is to live tranquilly with your husband." Then she laughed and said that she and her husband were very content together. I asked if she had chosen her husband or if he had chosen her. "Both of us. . . we chose each other." She laughed again. They had been married when Juan was twenty-two and she was seventeen, but she said that they had fallen in love five years before that. "Since school. We would have games together, playing, we didn't know." Then they became serious about each other, but had to wait until she was of age since her family wouldn't permit her to marry early. "Then we exchanged presents, the father-in-law and mother-in-law came to meet my father and mother. The *relleno* (special stuffing) was made." I asked if she was going to pick a wife for Jaime and Tomás, or if she would let them choose. "No, they will choose," she laughed. Jaime told me he already had the girl picked out, and he and his mother laughed together.

I asked Berta what she thought about punishment, and if she had ever hit her children. Her reply was unusual. "No. I never hit my children. It would hurt them. . ." So I asked Jaime if he had ever gone against the wishes of his mother on any important matter. "Yes, a few times. When I stayed out late and she didn't give me permission. . ." Berta, however, said that never in her life had she gone against her parent's wishes in anything. She felt that if you taught your children properly they would obey you. "And without hitting them, only with scoldings, gentle scoldings. . ." I wondered what her opinion was of the mothers in Chan Kom who had different ideas, but the only person she commented on was Anita. "She does not treat her children well. She doesn't train them. They throw stones. Of course, she is from a different village. Maybe that is why."

Beside their view on punishment, another thing which impressed me about the Pituh family was their strong emphasis on education. This had been made clear in a number of ways, and when I asked them the Fromm question on feeling superior to other people in any way, Jaime answered that they were superior in education. I mentioned that Don Trini was also very interested in education. But he had not sent his sons away for more schooling even though all said they had wanted to go, and had in fact been encouraged to do so by teachers and friends. One of his sons, Clemente, had run away from home at age twelve to attend school in Mérida. Berta's eldest son Tomás, on the other hand, had graduated from the *primaria* and was now attending the federal high school in Mérida. Jaime had gone to a special boarding school for Mayans in Balum Tum, and then on to the secondaria in Mérida. "We are the only ones," said Berta. "We want to have our children advance in their studying." I asked if she thought that her father was an influ-

ence in this matter, since he was widely traveled and had worked so
long for the cultural mission. She said yes, but that her husband was
also very interested in education; he wanted his children to get ahead
(un poco adelante).

We talked about her children some more, and I asked if she was
content with her life.

> We are happy. We are happy when there is a visitor for us to talk with,
> when we are tranquil together. Yes, we are satisfied. The children are
> getting ahead and we are content.

And they did seem that way to me. They are a very close, very loving
family. The children seem to have absorbed all their parents' en-
thusiasm for education. Even one of the songs the little girl sang for
me (with some prodding from Jaime), *"Papacito Me Siento Contento,"*
was about a child going happily off to school, knowing that this would
make a secure future. When asked to name the most important virtues,
Berta and Jaime both chose discipline, joy, and respect for others.

Later on, when we were talking about Don Juan's property in Chan
Kom, I learned that he had recently bought some land in Merida and
was intending to build a house for his children there. I wondered if
they were going to sell their house in Chan Kom. "No. Where would
all of our children live? They would have no place to go," Berta
answered. I asked them how they planned to divide the property between their seven children. "Equally," she said emphatically. "Equal
to daughter and to son." I learned that they like Chan Kom and Mérida
about the same, not feeling tied down to either place. But they are
definitely more city-oriented. They have no interest in living in the
mountains the way some of the people in Chan Kom have done, and
have not built a Mayan hut on their *milpa* like the Mecabs. They do
continue to plant and harvest, while many of the families in Chan Kom
have stopped making *milpa.* Perhaps they feel that one of their sons
will wish to continue using the *ejido* property to make his living. The
house in Mérida could be for those children who decide to leave Chan
Kom. Everything they do is in some way related to what they want for
their children. "For the children," said Berta, "I want them to learn
so we will get ahead. For them."

As I left, I thought I had begun to understand at least some of the
reasons why the Pituh family was so distinct from the others. I had
come to feel more positively about Berta and her family. Her relationship with her husband seemed a close one, and the whole family
radiated a loving, happy atmosphere. Even so, I never experienced the
same easy rapport which had come so naturally with my other friends

in Chan Kom. Partly, I think I felt that I somehow was being used by them, almost as an educational tool. But they would have been interested in any visitor in exactly the same way—to learn something, for the children to "advance a little," as Berta says. However, our relationship was perhaps further complicated by the fact that I was staying with the Mecabs and had been interviewing them primarily. Some of the old resentments might still linger.

They had asked that when I left I would stop by their house in Mérida. "Take our greetings. They would like to meet you, to talk with you." I remembered that Alfonso Villa Rojas had told me that the last time he was in Mérida at their home, he had been offered a scotch and soda, served with ice from the refrigerator. The jump from Chan Kom to Mérida, from Mecab to Mendoza, seemed enormous. I wondered if the Pituhs were an example of the family in transition which would perhaps come to be common in Chan Kom, or if the people there would be more jealous of their own customs and manners, and perhaps be more resistant to change.

3

Analysis of Data

Self-image: Appearance, Dress and Projection

Now that you have met the women of Chan Kom I would like to tell you more about what they wore and what they looked like. All of the wives in my network of friends except Flora and Berta still wore the traditional *huipil* and had long hair. The *huipil* is a white loose-fitting cotton dress, usually the same width from the top to the bottom, sewn at the sides with holes for arms and neck. This can be embroidered either by hand or by machine in geometrical cross-stitch or gaily flowered patterns. The neck opening and the bottom of the garment are usually embroidered, but sometimes there is only tucking along the armholes. The amount of decoration and the design varies from town to town and also from use for fiesta to use for daily work. This garment, although much less decorated or embroidered, is almost certainly a survival from ancient times and can be seen in frescoes and in the codices. When the detailed frescoes were discovered at Bonampak, people were amazed and surprised to see women present at the ritual ceremonies with the priests and rulers. It had been assumed by many that women were excluded! Underneath the *huipil* was and is worn a "midi" petticoat which has an embroidered bottom usually eyelet, sometimes tucked. Interesting too is the fact that the *huipil* in the frescoes was similar to the ones worn today. The only difference between the clothing of priestesses, queens, and the simple folk was in the elaborateness of the decoration and the quality of fabric being cotton or henequen.

The Mayan women also wear a *reboza* (in Mayan: *booch).* a long shawl which is draped different ways at different times, similar to the folded kerchief of *manta (pati)* which was used in ancient times.

That women wore the same sandals as men can be seen in the frescoes and designs. The sandals were bound to the feet by two thongs, one passing between the first and second toe, the other between the third and fourth toes. Today only the first of these thongs is still used by the men, and women use no sandals at all. At home they go barefooted, and for dress-up they wear European-style slippers, often made of plastic. Black, white, pink and blue are favorite colors in Chan Kom.

In 1940 the wife of the village school teacher demanded that all girls bob their hair and wear dresses to school. This caused mixed reactions, some families complying and some vehemently refusing. In 1948, only eight to ten teen-aged girls wore dresses, one woman wore a dress, and no one had bobbed hair. Most of the women and many of the girls still wear their black hair long, and keep it immaculately clean. Ana shampooed hers every third day in the water trough where she did her laundry. She usually would leave her hair loose, but would brush it up for special occasions and decorate it with bright ribbons and flowers. Some of the women, including Berta, have not only cut their hair but have permanents as well. The local beauty parlor is a three-legged stool set up outside a thatched hut. A front permanent costs only five pesos. The beautician said the cost of a full one depends on how much of the ointment purchased in Valladolid is used. The permanent on the Mayan women looked very unnatural and unbecoming to me, but are of course one of the prices of modernization.

As I think about the two wives in the network who have discarded the *huipil* for daily use and have cut their hair, I am surprised that they are such opposites. Flora is the least literate of the women, the least interested in her children's learning; Berta is the most knowledgeable, the most educated, and most ambitious for her family's education. One does not encourage, indeed often prevents her children from attending the local school, while the other has sent one child away to boarding school and the other to live with grandparents in order to attend school in the capital. One is sexually provocative, by Mayan standards, wearing a very low-cut fitted dress, while the other's dress has a similar design, but with a higher neck and much less body fit. Redfield noted that "some husbands' parents did not want their daughters to discard the *huipil* because they would no longer help with the *milpa*" (Redfield, 1950, p. 39). Flora said she wore modern dress because her husband thought it was *de mas categoria* (more stylish).

All the other women, however, pointed out various reasons for prefering the *huipil* to modern dress. So unbecoming to most foreigners, it seems to have been designed for the Mayan woman. Ana said she liked to wear the *huipil* "because the cool air refreshes my body." She added that she would not mind wearing a dress like mine, a comfortable drip-dry skirt and blouse, but that she would not want to wear dresses like the women in Mérida because they were too tight to be comfortable in getting on or off a bus, or to sit down to make tortillas.

In Chan Kom most of the young girls, but not all, had given up wearing the *huipil* to be dressed in a more fitted shift, and had discarded the petticoat hanging below. Result: a mini- *huipil!* The adolescent girl I noticed first wearing this mini- *huipil* had spent some time in Mérida with Beatriz. This was an interesting change from traditional to modern. Almost all the women, when dressing for photographs, put on the tight modern dresses of brightly colored cotton or rayon. Some had started using the redesigned *huipil,* and all of them wore plastic sandals or leather pumps to dress up. Later, when they saw that we liked the *huipil,* even preferred it, they posed for photos in their *huipiles.*

Some people would describe the Mayan women as short and stocky. The average height is four feet eight inches. According to Morley, they are one of the most broad headed people in the world with the cephalic index at 86.8 (Morley, 1946, p. 23). In fact, Waldeck thought the Maya "might be the 'missing link' between man and monkey." (Villa Rojas, 1969, p. 250). Many say the Mayan women look oriental. There is good evidence which suggests a northeastern Asiatic origin, since it is not uncommon for the modern Mayan to have the epicanthic eye fold and the Mongolian spot (Morley, 1946, p. 34). Their tawny golden-brown skin is smooth and shiny. Their hands are delicate, their fingers long, thin, and graceful, with their nails clean and seemingly manicured.

> the women are both physically and mentally superior to the men, and when dressed in gala costumes for a '*baile,*' wore spotlessly clean, beautifully embroidered garments, all of the gold ornaments they possess or can borrow, and often a coronet of fire beetles, looking like small electric lights in their hair; they present a very attractive picture. They are polite and hospitable, though rather shy with strangers. They are fond of gossip, and appreciate a joke, especially one of a practical nature.

This is from a 1918 Smithsonian publication (p. 16) by Thomas Gann on the Mayan Indians of Southern Yucatan. He somehow conveyed the feeling of beauty and dignity which so impressed me. I never saw a coronet of fire beetles, but I can imagine them in the elegant times of the past. I did see everything else he described and was pleased to come across this account written by a man so long ago.

After my first trip to Chan Kom I became aware of the feeling of beauty I had about the woman. I wondered if there was actually some sort of "aura," a feeling of self-beauty which they projected and I perceived. I decided to try to capture on film this "aura," or was it animation reflecting the joy and rhythm of their daily life? On my next visit to the village I brought a small camera, and found that the women were delighted to do a movie with me. Later, comparing the moving film of these people with still pictures, I was struck by the difference in the way an individual appeared in each. The beauty of the women is so apparent when one is with them or sees them animated, while in still photos they can seem rather dull. Perhaps their beauty *is* an "aura" which comes more from *their* feelings, self-images of being beautiful, rather than from any absolute quality of their physical structure.

In Las Cuevas, a *mestizo* village in central Mexico, Fromm and Maccoby (1970, p. 37) noted "the constant work that prematurely ages the peasant women." I had expected to find the same in Chan Kom, but in fact found almost an agelessness. A large part of the concept of time and age is on an annual basis, tied to the planting of corn, the ripening of fruits, the annual fiestas and even to the days of the births and deaths of family and friends (but not the years). People seldom if ever remember the year of an event but always the day and the month. The *exact* times and ages of things are unimportant to them. Years are lived, not added. William Herman adds this quality as one of the characteristics of their "good life." I had a great deal of difficulty determining peoples' ages. For instance, when I asked the widow Gabriela how old she was she replied, "I? Who knows, Señora? I must be seventy or sixty." But her son, Guillermo, and I were dubious. We started figuring back from the age of his birth.

"How old were you when you married, Gabriela?"

"Fifteen. It was on the fifteenth of October."

"And when you had Guillermo, your first child?"

"It was about two or three years later—I must have been eighteen."

"How old are you, Guillermo?"

"I don't know. Maybe twenty-eight."

"How old were you when you married?"

"I don't know. I had just finished military service—I had marched for a year."

"You were nineteen and that was six years ago. So you're twenty-five. And that makes Gabriela only forty-three."

"I'm only forty-three!"

"Yes, you're ten years younger than I am."

"Ten years, Señora. It's almost the same," she laughed.

In a few minutes we had removed twenty years from her age. At forty-four she is a good-looking woman, in spite of working the *milpa* "like a man." Indeed, I found beauty and vigor in all of the women, even in Luz who has worked more or less as a servant all of her life, yet seems to have endless energy. The faces of the women in their thirties and forties are amazingly smooth and taut, and their black hair glistens without any show of white. As I talked with these women I wondered about Steggerda's report in which he said that "the Mayan woman reaches maturity at fifteen and then has 'seventeen years of reproductive life" (Steggerda, 1941, p. 216). This would mean that by thirty-two, Mayan women have reached menopause, finished their child-bearing years. Most of the girls and women said their first menses were between thirteen and fourteen, and there were women in their thirties and at least one in her early forties who asked me about birth control. Are the women in this village different from the sample Steggerda used or is this a changing pattern? From my limited sample and data I cannot answer; I can say that in spite of heavy work and many children, the women remain vigorous and attractive, and have not aged prematurely.

Age is always difficult to evaluate in another culture, and obviously the people in Chan Kom had problems determining our ages. One thought a fellow field-worker two years younger than I was my daughter, and another asked if a student field assistant, more than thirty years younger, was my husband.

Family and Home: Marriage and Children

How do the women feel about their lives? Are they happy? The words they use are *satisfecha con la vida* —satisfied with life. I had asked various people a question suggested to me by Erich Fromm: "How do you feel about your life? Are you very satisfied, a little satisfied, dissatisfied." Almost unanimously, the answer was *"muy satisfecha."* The women feel they are happy, and they radiate this feeling. All but the oldest seem happy with their husbands; perhaps she is also, but it is a strange relationship to me. The others all told me that they loved their husbands, in spite of the fact that all except two had married the persons who had been chosen for them by their fathers.

Bishop de Landa stated that formerly the Maya married at twenty

years of age, but in the sixteenth century they married when they were
twelve or fourteen (Tozzer, 1941, p. 209). In the eighteenth and early
nineteenth centuries, Maya boys of Yucatan married at about seventeen or eighteen and girls between fourteen or fifteen. Today in the
Indian villages of the Northern peninsula, the average age of the boys
at marriage is twenty-one and of the girls, nearly seventeen. Seventeen
still seems a very accepted age for marriage for girls in Chan Kom.
According to this same study both male and female are considered
mature at fifteen. Villa Rojas observed:

> Marriages are arranged by parents, boy's parents taking the initiative. On
> the last visit, when everything has been arranged between the parents, the
> girl is consulted, 'for no one ought to be married by force' but very rarely
> does the girl oppose the decision of her parents.

Certainly none of the women I talked with had considered not obey-
ing their fathers in this matter. Again according to Villa Rojas:

> The qualities sought in a woman are youth, good health, and a serious
> disposition. It is thought that a woman who laughs too easily or talks too
> much is inclined to laziness and is susceptible to amatory advances.
>
> (Villa Rojas, 1945, p. 87)

Most men would also include diligence as a desirable characteristic.
In Chan Kom, where one village leader has a very strong feeling about
color, girls with light complexions are favored. According to Morley,

> The fathers took great care to find suitable wives for their sons, preferably
> girls of the same social class and of the same village. Certain relationship
> taboos existed. It was considered wicked to marry a girl who had the same
> surname, though first cousin marriages were not forbidden.
>
> (Morley, 1956, p. 168)

In Chan Kom, however, we observed a number of people by the
same surname who had married, and several were also first cousins
once removed. (See chart in Appendix.)

The use of professional matchmakers, called in Mayan *ahatanzhob,*
had been common in Chan Kom in the thirties, but everyone said that
now the fathers of the boys made the decisions as to who married
whom. However, in talking to the husbands and wives I found that
some of the men had chosen the girls they wanted to marry and had
then asked their fathers to approve and go through the formalities.
These include the traditional exchange of gifts such as chocolate and
other foods.

Even today, during the period of engagement the man is often called
upon to feed his bride-to-be, and to provide all of her necessities. She
in turn must wash his clothes at the home of his parents. In Chan Kom

a man of thirty-two asked a father for his daughter who was only fourteen, agreeing to pay for her food for three years until she was seventeen. I did not ask whether she had washed his clothes during these three years, but as he was a traveling salesman who visited her town from time to time, perhaps she did so when he was there.

In Yucatan today, the groom or his family defrays all expenses of the wedding, including the bride's trousseau. The boy's mother often makes clothing for her son and daughter-in-law, but more and more they go together to buy it in the nearest market town. After marriage the bride may live with her in-laws, and "When this happens the girl is called *ilibtzil.* . . If the groom goes to live with the bride's parents he is called *hauncabzil."* (Steggerda, 1941, p. 147) Since there are Mayan names for both of these practices, there would appear to be no fixed pattern of preference. However, all of Don Trini's sons have lived with him during the first years of their married lives. Now all but one have set up separate households.

In the thirties when there was a strong socialist party in Yucatan, there were polygamous families reported in various villages, including three in Chan Kom. In all of these cases a single household was maintained, with the second wife playing the subordinate role. Even under these circumstances, the man seems to expect sexual fidelity of his wife. It has been observed, however, that virginity is not required in a bride (Redfield, Villa Rojas, 1934, p. 96). Pre-marital sexual relations seem to be rare, but according to Villa Rojas, an increased number of babies were being born out of wedlock in the forties. When he asked Don Trini the reason, the answer was "The nixtemal." "How?" asked Villa Rojas, "that's strange." Don Trini told him "The *nixtamal* starts early, and so women go out before dawn to grind their own corn the way they used to at home. They meet the boys in the dark, and that's why illegitimacy is caused by the *nixtamal."* He went on to say that all of his younger sons had premarital sexual relations. One of them, in fact, although he is married, has several children by another woman in the village and still visits her on occasion.

Except in the case of one woman, there was no talk of mistresses or promiscuity in the town by the women. This woman told me that several of the men, including husbands of some of the women I was interviewing, went to this one house in town where, as she said, they carried on *porquerias.* According to Gann, it was

> . . . highly immoral for a married man to have a mistress. For each year a horn will grow out of his soul, so his soul cannot get to heaven through the narrow window, and will return to earth as the wind that blows over the *milpa* at times of burning.
>
> (Gann, 1918, p. 59)

I never heard any stories of personal vendettas or cruel punishment taken against unfaithful wives or husbands such as Steggerda found in other Mayan towns. He reported at length some very extreme examples of such actions, from heavy beating to stoning the offender to death (Steggerda, 1941, p. 52-55). I do not think he was insinuating that this was a norm, however, and does say toward the end that "this jealousy and retaliation is not always characteristic of the Maya" *(Ibid., p. 54)*. Sex behavior among the Maya does not play an overly important part. Marriage is expected of couples living together, even widows and widowers. Incest is not common, and rape is practically unknown *(Ibid., p. 87)*.

It is often true that the modern day Maya marry without love in the modern American sense. It seems rather a matter of routine. The boy wants a home and children of his own, so either his parents or a matchmaker simply arrange for this marriage with a suitable girl (Morely, 1956, p. 168).

There are exceptions, of course, today as in times past. Villa Rojas reported the marriage of a couple, the bridegroom so poor that he lacked even enough money for a religious ceremony. The bride had been discouraged from marrying the man, yet she was so determined in her love for him that she responded to remarks about his poverty by saying that it did not matter, since "they could live in the shade of a tree" (Redfield/Villa Rojas, 1934, p. 246).

Within the context of the stable and functional social structure of Chan Kom, dyadic marriage has a very firm niche. Married women seem happy in the married state, and unquestioning of it; they seem to feel for their daughters that this is the only way a woman would want to live. Evans-Prichard (1965, p. 16) put it rather matter-of-factly in his book *The Position of Women in Primitve Societies:*

> After all, marriage is not simply a relation between man and woman as males and females. It is, of course, that, but it is also much more, a mutual adjustment of individuals in a *certain social relationship.*

Villa Rojas said that he had noticed in Quintana Roo, and I felt the same in Chan Kom, that couples are very stable and usually pass their lives together in congenial and tranquil companionship.

> Quarrels are very rare and the small disagreements which do occur are brief and inconspicuous. During the course of his time in Quintana Roo only once did he see an instance when a man struck his wife, and in no instance did a wife strike a husband.
>
> (Villa Rojas, 1954, p. 89)

Even though the young do not make arrangements for their own weddings in traditional societies,

> Love in our sense of the word undoubtedly exists between a large number
> of Maya couples, probably as large a population as among Europeans.
> The boy who was unknown before the marriage later became the lover.
>   (Thompson, 1954, p. 153)

Of the ten couples that I got to know well in Chan Kom, eight seemed to be "loving partners," by the Fromm/Maccoby definition. In the village they studied they found very few husbands and wives who could fit the definition, and those few were considered by the others as "remarkable, admirable, but exceptional" (Fromm/Maccoby, 1970, p. 149).

But then they also found strong *machismo* feelings among the men, as is common throughout Mexico. *"Machismo* indicates an attitude of male superiority, a wish to control women and keep them in an inferior position" *(Ibid.,* p. 266). In Chan Kom I found very little of this attitude. In fact, many social scientists have found less *machismo* in Indian communities than in *mestizo* communities. While the village is set up as a patriarchy, with the men holding the positions of power, they treat their wives and children with love, concern, and respect. They are not a demonstrative people, however. "In the years in Yucatan I never saw even an overt sign of affection, not even an arm around a shoulder or a hand touching. Husband and wife would pass each other on the plaza without speaking, but there may have been signals I did not understand. Or, as John Elmendorf suggested, passing in the plaza is rather like meeting in the hall of your home. Both husbands and wives agreed that it was more important for a wife to be loving than it was for her to keep the home clean and orderly, except for Doña Victoria, who believes the other way around. Don Trini told me, "If a wife is loving, she will keep the house clean and orderly." In their homes there is a very warm interpersonal relationship, and gradually I was accepted into this intimate feeling with husbands and wives and children. Husbands and wives sit together around the hearth on low stools, talking, drinking chocolate or cola. When tortillas are being made, the woman continues doing this while her husband and children eat. There does not seem to be the rigid segregation of males and females at eating in the nuclear family, as is often reported in the ethnographies, except in Don Trini's large family where more than one nuclear group eats together. Although a female, I was considered primarily an outsider, and was expected to sit at the table with the men when eating at Don Trini's. This was also true of the female teachers when the governor made his visit.

In Chan Kom, the life of a family is such that to be childless is to have a very lonely, empty life. In fact, two of the three divorces granted since

1940 were because *no tuvieron niños* (they had no children). One couple had only been married for a month and sixteen days! Ann Macias (1971) states that to be barren in pre-Columbian times was cause for divorce. But forty-six days does not seem to be a long enough time to have established this to be the case. There have been separations, but these have been informal. It is generally true in Chan Kom, as Jane Fishburne Collier observed in Zinacantan, "that women are able to live without husbands far more easily than men are able to live without wives" (Collier, 1973, p. 199).

The mothers' faces show signs of great fatigue, as they stand through long ceremonies with nursing babies or a baby in the *rebozo,* as younger children cling to their skirts or hands. But only once have I seen a mother leave a crying child alone uncuddled. On more than one occasion I saw fathers holding their children, both boys and girls, with heads against their knees, patting them lovingly while they continued to talk with friends. While the men sit around the plaza at dusk, their young children leave the groups they play in from time to time and sit quietly with their fathers or uncles. Children are loved and they know it. They exude happiness and freedom. The seeming lack of both punishment and formal guidance from parents astounded me. Even toddlers near the open hearth were not cautioned, nor did they seem to need to be. I thought of the folk song Ana sang about the *ratoncita* —the little rat who burned her hand on the bean pot, and then she knew that it was hot. The mother rat made her hand well, but she had not warned or forbidden. This seemed the way for children to learn too. When I asked any of the adults how many times they had disobeyed their parents, except for one instance the answer was always "never." This seemed remarkable, but apparently is the accepted way.

"Even at an early age, children sincerely respect the wishes and rights of their mothers. Mothers love their infants, and abortion and infanticide are relatively unknown" (Steggerda, 1941, p. 87). Caring for the children is a shared task among the women in families, and older siblings are often assigned to take care of a specific child. For example, in the extended family in which I was living, each older daughter took care of one of her two younger brothers, and each felt a special relationship to that brother. I noticed older women referred to younger siblings as "the one I used to take care of," and even children were proudly possessive of the achievements and exploits of younger brothers and sisters who had been their special responsibility. Children are very merry, at ease with all ages and both sexes. And as both boys and girls care for their younger relatives, often of the opposite sex, this helps break down the "division" by sex.

According to the ethnographies and to the women themselves, girls and boys play separately except when they are very small. However, I personally observed many instances of group play. The plaza is like a big playground or community room; there is a great deal of cheerful pushing and chasing, as well as some crying on the part of the younger children. Even nursing babies were a part of this larger play group, riding on their mothers' or siblings' hips. One of the favorite games is rolling a hoop made from a circle of vines. On the left hand side of the plaza is the baseball diamond which the Rural Cultural Mission introduced to the village in 1946. The sport has stayed a favorite in spite of the fact that Don Trini seems to think it a waste of time; clothes get dirty and you earn nothing. (On my July visit, Chan Kom had just won games with Xochenpich and Pisté and was about to play a "championship" game that Sunday on a new diamond playing field being fixed at the entrance to the town.)

Little children tied June bugs on strings and swung them around, just as we had done as children in the South. Green fruits were tied to a string and danced like spinning tops. Children pulled stones or blocks of wood around on strings, making noises like cars. One of the boys made animals with local clay and baked them in the sun. As I passed through Flora's house in the evening her nine-year-old daughter was often playing with paper dolls by candlelight on the floor with her little brother, constructing make-believe clothes from rags, papers, or leaves. They were very creative about using natural objects as toys. Sometimes this meant that dogs or chickens were treated very cruelly, being dragged or beaten or chased, as they became horses or tigers. As in all parts of Mexico, animals, especially dogs, are brutally treated, not just by the children but by all ages.

Both boys and girls especially liked singing to the tape recorder and hearing it played back. Many of the songs had to do with animals and simple household tasks, but I heard no love songs at all from either adults or children.

Mothers seemed to have lots of time to sit in their hammocks, their children swinging in hammocks nearby. While the women sewed the young girls would be practicing their embroidery, or just playing with needles and thread. There is no proscribed, formal teaching by mothers and fathers as reported by Hellblom in her analysis of the Aztec codices (1973). But there is a definite sense of responsibility to teach and share skills with one's children. This knowledge of certain skills—making *huipiles,* tortillas, finding herbs, and so on—is expected of young girls by a certain age.

Another aspect of the non-directive approach to child raising is evident in the traditional attitude towards menstruation. The mothers all said that it was a sin to tell a daughter ahead of time about menses, and that when they started the daughters would come to you and then you would explain. When I asked if this was not frightening, the mothers said yes, but this was the way it was done. One other thing I had not previously tied to menstrual periods in my thinking was that girls are not allowed to go to school after they are twelve. According to one mother, this was because once you had your menstrual period, it was not good to be in the same school with boys. It is around this age that there is a real separation by sex in play. But just as there is no talk about the menstruation before the fact, there is likewise no discussion of this separation of playing by sexes. They seem to know by example rather than instruction.

Although the women talked with me frankly and openly about menstruation, birth control and other aspects of female sexuality, any discussion of sex relations with males seemed taboo. It may well be that linguistic problems were the root of this problem, that I did not know their words for such a discussion, that perhaps they used only Mayan when discussing such matters.

As I mentioned earlier, the women spoke Mayan as their first language. In fact, even though they knew I spoke no Mayan at all (or sometimes because of it?), they slipped into Mayan whenever men were around, or when it seemed they wanted to check a point or conceal a statememt, and always when they were sitting together in their tortilla-making circles. I always wondered what they were saying behind my linguistic back. From the laughter it was obvious they were telling jokes, or kidding each other in some way. When I checked with Villa Rojas later, he told me that when sitting in their circles they gossiped, told jokes, and played, and that probably at times the conversation was filled with double entendres and talk of sex. He asked if I had ever seen them play the "needle game," which he described in his journal and which they still enjoy. Unfortunately I never did. It sounded like a lot of fun to watch. It is supposed to be a way in which one can "learn their fate" by playing with needles.

> In a gourd vessel filled with water they carefully place two needles, taking care that they do not sink. Then they name them with the names of persons who want to know their fate, properly a young man and a girl. If the needles come together, a marriage is indicated; if one immediately sinks, the person represented will die, and if on the contrary it remains a long time without sinking, it is a sign of a prosperous and happy life.
> (Redfield/Villa Rojas, 1934, p. 251)

Most of the women of Chan have five to nine children, making the average family there slightly larger than the national average of 6.6 (Elu, 1969, p. 77). When asked how many children they had or how many they wanted, all of the women except one countered by asking me how many children I had. When I said two, they asked how we only had two children, and how Americans know how not to have more. This seemed to be an interest of theirs which, as I came to know them better, we could discuss freely and in depth. All but one said they hoped to go to a nearby village to visit a Mayan doctor whom I knew, one trained by Planned Parenthood in birth control methods, including IUDs. In one of my early visits, Don Trini suggested that I talk with the women about birth control. His understanding and the freedom with which he discussed such matters with me seemed extremely rare. He was pleased, but surprised, when I told him that most of them had already asked me for information. Alphonso Villa Rojas had reported that "proudly they turned down the use of contraceptives" in the thirties when he suggested to the men that there were protective devices that they could use so as to have fewer children. But then, that was when the men were to take the precautions.

I have read many studies in which various suggestions have been made for making Birth Control in Family Planning programs more effective, but none proposes to approach it from the standpoint of a human right (to have or not to have children) rather than economic and environmental considerations. I feel strongly that motivational programs should be related to human rights and women's rights, not just world needs, and also that cultural differences be taken into account as we consider the limits of growth and the quality of human life.

So far I have given the women information only about birth control and ways to learn about it. I did not feel I should do more than this, nor did I feel I could do less. Women whom I did not know came up to me asking if I could share with them information about not having more children because they did not want more babies. Some also approached my student field assistant, a young woman, so their questions were not just limited to me as an older known person, but also as a woman.

The midwife whom I mentioned earlier was one of the most important women in Chan Kom because of her supposed birth control abilities. Several women claimed to have been "fixed" by her so that they would have no more children, although she herself would not admit to this. Doña Concepción is one of the most beautiful women I had ever seen, with great dignity and presence. When she was thirty, thirty-five years ago, she became a midwife, but not by apprenticing herself. She learned everything through dreams. Doña Concepción told me that she had never lost a patient if the mother had been with her for the regular massages, *hikab,* which begin in the third month. She uses almond oil and by massaging the entire body, she can move the baby and also prepare the mother's body for the birth.

Concepción also explained to me the importance of the father's role in childbirth. He must stand at the head of the hammock while the delivery takes place. With his hands over the sides he must clasp them under his wife's head at the nape of her neck so as to form a brace against which she could push during labor. In case of delay the husband passes under the hammock nine times and raises his wife each time with his back. As Kathryn MaKay, the nurse with the Carnegie Expedition, observed, the father always remains in the room until the baby is born, "because he was the one who gave the woman the child" (Redfield/Villa Rojas, 1934, p. 362).

However, when I asked if she knew how to help women who were afraid to have other babies, to prevent pregnancy, she said, "It would be a sin to try to control things like that, because God gives the menses and stops them. He starts them when a girl is twelve and stops them when she is fifty. To disturb this is a sin."

Economy, Property, and Income

Concerning property in Chan Kom, we should remember Redfield's observation:

> . . . to take residence in a Yucatecan pueblo is not simply to make one's house and home there. It is to become enrolled in a community of men enjoying common rights and subject to common obligations to obey the local authorities and especially to perform the labor required, regularly and also on special occasions, for the common good.
>
> (Redfield, 1951, p. 12)

This refers specifically to the rights and obligations of men. My own special interest was to see where women fit into the overall economy as owners, inheritors and manipulators of real and personal property.

When I discussed this question with Don Trini, who was *comisario ejidal* for the third time, he loaned me a book called *Las Derechas de la Mujer Campesina (Rights of Rural Women)* published in 1969 by Mexican congresswomen. I was struck by one sentence which read:

> Even though it may seem that her legal rights are not equal to those of men, perhaps the distinction is to the benefit of women, since her obliga-

tions as mother of young Mayans are and should have precedence over the obligations to work personally and directly the *parcela* (plot) which is the only requisite to keep it. But a woman had no right to ejido property if she had a husband—only widowed, divorced or unmarried.

This seemed a strange statement to me, but as Don Trini explained it this meant that women did not lose their property by not working it if they were taking care of their children but a man would in fact lose his unless he worked it. No one could sell *ejido* property; but by leaving it untended, one could lose it.

In 1926 Chan Kom was given formal possession of 2,400 *hectares* of communal property. Much of it was stony and barren, but there was great joy in the village at receiving enough land to be divided into *parcelas,* the individual plots of land which were allocated to individual to farm personally. As *comisario ejidal,* Don Trini has the right to assign these properties. He explained to me that every male citizen over eighteen has a right to 600 *mecates,* approximately five acres, of this *ejido* land. In fact, Don Trini added that widows or unmarried women also have this right, but very few of them exercise it.

Along with *ejido* property, there are town lots called *solares* or *predios.* These are assigned to new residents by the mayor, the *presidente municipal.* If these are undeveloped, they are free to the assignees, but if they have improvements such as walls, masonry buildings, or wells they can be sold by the town for the cost of the construction. These seem to vary in size, and some in the past have been bought back by the community to be reassigned or sold. When the Puucs and Hops left Chan Kom during the religious disputes of 1955, the town bought back their places. A number of people in Chan Kom own private property as well as their house lots, *solares* and *ejido* lands.

Doña Luz was the only woman other than the widow Gabriela who pointed out her *solar* to me. Not only did she take pride in owning her own property, but her grand-daughters always reminded me that such and such a *solar* belonged to Doña Luz. The other wives seemed to own their homes with their husbands, and thought of them as family property.

In addition to property which is owned, people have built homes. These are often the elliptical thatched huts built in the traditional Mayan way. Most of the houses built around the town square, however, are of masonry, usually just one room wide with a thatched hut in the back where meals are cooked and most of the family living takes place. Many of these houses were built by community effort at the time the village was trying to be declared a *pueblo.* Many times I have thought of these as facades, because the people use and enjoy their thatched huts more, but are proud of their masonry show-places. On my first visit, the Spanish-looking square seemed to me like a theatre set, with real life going on behind.

To give an example from my own experience, and to get back to the women, I would like to share a story that has to do with these homes. The night before the governor came to visit Chan Kom, Don Trini, the mayor, and two members of the town council were deeply involved in an angry conversation. Later I was told that the problem was over who would cook turkey to be served to the governor and where the official dinner would be held. Don Trini explained that it would be very nice if it could be in Pepe's house, because it was of masonry and had a tile floor and was "very modern," but Pepe had to find out whether or not it could be there, because *no sólo él manda* (he is not in charge alone). "It's still his mother's house. He's gone to ask her. Even though she cannot read, she is the one who gives the orders." Her son Pepe, a grown man with a family, a member of the town council, did not feel that he could invite the governor to his home without getting permission from his mother. In fact, the dinner was not held there, but in another home. Presumably Mother said no.

Animals are a real source of income for the women. They take care of the pigs, turkeys and chickens, and the money they get for this work is theirs. I am sure this is true in all cases except for the pigs, which seem often to be owned together but are traded by men. As for poultry, both turkeys and hens have to be purchased from the women by the men, even for such ceremonial occasions as the dinner for the governor. When Doña Luz sold a black turkey to her son-in-law, the mayor, for the governor's lunch, there were thirty minutes of careful examination and negotiation before a price was settled on. The young girls and women seem to feel very possessive of their animals, their cattle, chickens, and pigs, and they take great pride in breeding them, selling them, and having money of their own.

Vegetable gardens in the houses, which are still set up as hollow logs on forked sticks as they were in pre-Conquest times, are considered very much the property of the wives. They sell or barter chiles or tomatoes for other things they want. I watched *centavos* being given for lemons from the tree. They also sell other fruits, and Ana even sold water from the well to a visiting man and his horse.

Making hammocks and embroidering, both by hand and by machine, are major sources of pride and income for the women. It is considered very meritorious to know how to do the traditional cross-stitch. This results in the lovely embroidery which goes around the square neck and hem of the *huipil.* A girl is supposed to have made one before she is twelve. There is also great pride in designing new patterns, which, according to Victoria, is a very difficult thing to do. (She combines the traditional designs in new ways and creates flowers and birds from her imagination, all in vivid colors which she sews both by hand and by machine.)

In nearly all the houses, in both masonry buildings and the thatched huts, one sees mothers and daughters swinging in their hammocks, doing their cross-stitches as they chat. When neighbors drop by, they continue sewing, and often the neighbors will have brought along their own work to do.

Two of the wives I came to know well make embroidery to be sold. Many of the wives, both the ones I got to know and their children, make embroidery on strips which they sell to people who happen into the town, or in Chichen Itza, the nearby Mayan ruins which are heavily visited by national and international tourists. Some women in town seem to act as go-betweens and to take the embroidery in for their friends and neighbors.

Hammock-making too is a family activity, and a source of income for the women, who usually sell the finished product for twice the cost of the thread. It was amazing to me to see the unfinished hammock stretched on its upright loom with many colored threads and shuttles in baskets beside it. As husbands or children came in and out of the hut, they wove a few minutes—or a few inches—talking as they worked. Ana's husband, Jorge, now has a hammock frame stretched in the front room while she has one in the thatched hut. As complicated as the whole process looked to me, I never heard anyone give admonitions or instructions.

Ana takes great pride in her hammock-making. She told me the names of all the designs in her multicolored hammocks: there were butterflies, squirrels, flowers, birds, and even the newly created design of my dress pattern, called the Señora Maria which she had just woven. There is a real feeling of artistic competition between the different women, who often boast of the strength, intricacy or beauty of their work.

Still another traditonal handicraft carried on by women, but limited to a very few in Chan Kom, is the making of the *chuyub* (literally, gourd-carrier). Ana took me to visit her aunt and her daughter who sell baskets which they make from the bark of the *habin* tree, and then cover with dried strips of palm and henequen fibers in intricate geometric designs which are quite colorful, done mostly in green and

cerise. The importance of these little baskets, in addition to the money earned by their makers, is that they are used to carry gifts between people in various ceremonial ways, including the formal exchanges of gifts which are part of the marriage arrangements and the offerings to the Mayan gods.

There are still other and newer sources of income for the women of Chan Kom, some only recently added to the more or less traditional income-producing activities. In 1934 Redfield noted:

> Baking of bread in masonry ovens of a Spanish type is a man's trade in the city and the towns, and in Chan Kom too, all such baking is done by men.

> (Redfield/Villa Rojas, 1934, p. 71)

Later in 1950, Redfield again commented: Bread is baked once a week or oftener by each of two bakers, and several other men know how to bake and have built ovens. The first Chan Kom baker learned how to bake by watching an outsider who was paid to come down and bake bread in Chan Kom. During the years of drought (1942-43), five or six Chan Kom men baked wheat bread steadily to meet the needs of people deprived of corn. Now Chan Kom has become an exporter of the art as well as of the bread; on two recent occasions men of the village have gone to neighboring settlements to teach others there— for a fee—the art of bread-making.

> (Redfield, 1950, pp. 47-48)

The first time I met Amparo, she had just made 300 *pesos* in two days selling little sweet cakes baked in her great round oven, which takes up most of the space in her kitchen hut. Baked bread is a luxury, almost a mystery, and a source of income and status for Amparo and her daughters. To be sure, some men are still baking bread in Chan Kom, but as it is being taken over by such enterprising women as Amparo, it is no longer exclusively a male function.

Along with bread making and store tending there is another recent activity which women are taking over in Chan Kom. Ana runs one of the four *molinos de nixtamal* which was purchased by her husband, his father, and his brother. They all share in the profits, but Ana gets paid for running it, and keeps the money. She says that she makes about five *pesos* a day (150 *pesos* a month) from her *molino*. Often her first customers arrive before three in the morning. She leaves her hammock in the kitchen hut where she sleeps with her husband and son, and goes into the large masonry room in front, right on the plaza. "No I'm not afraid. I take my candle." And so, off and on for several hours, Ana's clients, mostly friends and relatives, come in to grind their corn before they make their morning tortillas. From before dawn until eight or nine o'clock, and again from four until dusk, Ana has to be available. Eight hours for sixty cents. But she receives people in the dark store front as though she were the maitre d' of a fancy restaurant. Often her customers start the motor, put the cover back and clean up—with help from the ever-present feeding turkeys—and then hand Ana the twenty *centavos*. She has done little more than look on during the whole process.

The money the women get from their work remains theirs. Some simply hide it. Some invest it in sewing machines or gold chains. The gold chains are worn daily with extra ones added for fiestas or other special occasions. Husbands buy gold chains for their brides when they get married and later as special gifts. The wearing of gold chains seems to be practically the only way to show wealth among the women of Chan Kom, since nearly everyone wears the same kind and quality of dress.

Great prestige can be gained by wearing gold chains. Some women wear as many as six. Even though husbands may have been adorning wives to show their wealth, I thought that most wives felt personally proud of their chains and saw them as their own property. In Villa Rojas's diary (Redfield/Villa Rojas, 1934, p. 237) there is an example of a man who, when charged by his creditors to pay his debts, hands them his wife's gold chains while he goes for the money. This was the Mayan equivalent of hocking the family jewels! If the wife ever leaves her husband, in most cases she takes her chains with her.

The ownership of cattle was—and still is—another indication of wealth. But this did not relate so specifically to the women, except for those few whom I have mentioned above, who had invested specifically and personally in cattle.

Some aspects of the way money is dealt with and handled are illustrated in the events which transpired with Ana, the woman who was very ill on my second visit to Chan Kom. When her husband refused to take her to the clinic, she informed him that she would go alone if necessary, and use her own money. With this threat of a public demonstration of her personal and fiscal independence her husband sold two pigs and took her to the clinic. This incident, along with others I observed, made me realize that the women did have more freedom to control their lives than I had thought or read about previously. The property which they own or the things which they can sell do in fact give them money which is theirs to spend as they wish, and they take real pride in the freedom this gives them.

The question of "freedom" in the context of Chan Kom takes on several dimensions. We have seen above, for example, that men think women's work is harder and women say that men's work is harder. One element involved in this apparent contradiction seems to be that men perceive women's work as being confining, limited to the house and yard, while theirs is free of that constricting element. Women see men's work as being harsh, physically exhausting and therefore not as free as is theirs, since men do not have the opportunity to take advantage of free moments in the hammock, in the coolness of the home. What we have, then, is a reverse pair of concepts, one involving freedom *to* and the other freedom *from*. There would appear to be little difference in the value assigned by the women to their freedom to enjoy what the men perceive as limiting factors and that which the men assign to their freedom of movement, in turn seen by the women as limiting or negative factors. Thus, both men and women *feel* freer and consequently live in a value system which is more comfortable for them, using their freedoms in ways which enhance their respective joy in life and hence the overall harmony of their lives together. Another dimension of the relative freedom of men and women may derive from the phenomenon commented on by Oscar Lewis. He was referring to Tepoztlan, but I have noted the same thing in Chan Kom. "In general," he says, "women's work is less rigidly defined than men's" (Lewis, 1969, p. 25). I have elsewhere commented on the almost random *appearance* of structure in the daily routines of the women, their occasional "hammock-breaks," their sporadic turns at the loom or at embroidery and their unscheduled lives, with little other than the preparation of meals to demand a specific action at a specific time and that are not tied down to an hour. But there is some evidence that activities were once the exclusive domain of the men, activities which do indeed demand a more rigid structure, which are increasingly becoming open to the women of Chan Kom. Among these tasks are the baking of bread for sale, keeping shop, and even the singing of sacred songs, once the exclusive role of the *maestro cantor,* now being assumed by the *rezoneras.* In other words, as Lewis noted earlier, women are much freer to redefine their roles than men (Lewis, 1969, p. 25).

Another kind of freedom they have comes from the very process of selling embroidery, which they often carry into the neighboring town of Chichen Itza. Some of them consider this two and one half hours walk a pleasant jaunt. In fact, some of the women have started buying embroidery from others and acting as middlewomen. On the governor's visit, with the new road opening up, a number of the women talked of setting up a marketing cooperative where they could sell their wares.

In summary, even though the amount of cash income is very nominal, there is much more feeling of independence on the part of these women than I have sensed among many women in the United States. Dorothy Lee has said, "Self-esteem is paramount and rests on freedom and self dependence" (Lee, 1959, p. 160). The women of Chan Kom derive self-esteem from their essential skills and knowledge, and from their private income, possessions, livestock, and real property. The combination of these assets places them in an integral position in the functioning of the village economy and in their homes. They also take great joy in sharing their knowledge and skills with their children. One reason Victoria gave for wanting a daughter was that she wanted to teach her all the things she knew.

Work, Religion, and Nature

As I talked about women and their property rights, and their income from selling their handicrafts or their produce and livestock, I saw that these activities gave them a feeling of self worth, of independence and freedom. But along with these activities, parts of which might be considered optional, there are other duties which are strictly defined for wives, as there are specific duties for husbands. Just as "to live with a woman, to make *milpa,* to bring home enough corn and cash to feed, clothe and house the family" might be a man's definition of marriage, so, according to Redfield, "to live with a man, to make his tortillas and wash his clothes, is very nearly a women's definition of a marriage" (Redfield/Villa Rojas, 1934, p. 97). He could have also added to bear the children, because children are very much desired by both men and women. But as we have discussed above, village women want birth control information so they will only have to bear wanted children, or at least be released from the fear of multiple pregnancies.

Certainly "to make his tortillas and wash his clothes" is expected of every wife. The number of hours spent by a woman on laundry varies depending on how many males there are in the family and how many daughters to help. After filling the earthen jugs and metal drums with water near the corner of the hut where the three stones are grouped for hearth fires, the women start laundering the family clothes in long troughs made of hewn wood, or sometimes of plastic but in the original design and color. These laundry areas are placed in the shade under flowering trees, often between the thatched hut and the masonry front room (if it is a two room house). This chore, too, is done with pride. Getting the *huipiles* and the shirts snowy white is a domestic science, since the women use ashes from the hearth fire, some leaves now and then, packaged soap, and careful sunning. The women continue washing as they chat with family and friends, and their children play nearby.

Every day when the husbands come home from work in the field or even from the plaza, they expect warm water and clean clothes. The water for their warm bath is a part of those forty to fifty pails a day the women draw from the deep weels. Before the women can begin to heat water or make tortillas they must have kindling to burn in the hearth. To see Luz coming in with a tump line on her forehead carrying an enormous load of kindling disturbed me. In fact I asked her son why he did not help his elderly mother. "She likes to *leñar,*" he said. And when she invited me to go with her I accepted. Even though the chiggers *(garapatas)* were voracious the woods were cool, and we had a botanical field trip. In her shoulder bag *(sabucan)* she dropped leaves and roots which she cut and dug with her sickle, a small sharp machete. As she worked she told me the name and medical use of each plant. She is well known as an herbalist *(curandera),* and her time to *leñar* is her time to collect. Her grandchildren, both boys and girls, are allowed to go with her, but only if they bring their tump line and return with wood. Some of the other wives gather wood, others do not, and some husbands and sons keep their family hearths stocked. As an English speaking Mayan friend has told me,

> I grew up in a Yucatecan village. I remember when I went with my mother and friends for wood. . . . Even though wood is needed very often, somehow carrying it has taken on a different meaning for me. I no longer see this as man's work being done by women and children, I see it as truly a game, a sport, an outing.

I can only partially agree with the general belief of many male ethnographers, stated specifically by Redfield, that "a woman's sphere is about the home and her activities are always private, whereas a man's occupied in the field and forest, and his activities are often public" (Redfield/Villa Rojas, 1934, p. 68). However, women appear a great deal going across the plaza to get their corn ground or draw their water, or on their way to the woods to gather kindling. In fact I often wondered if they felt the water was light because, although it was heavy work and hard work, it was still a pleasure to see each other, talk, and be out of the house for a while. In addition, most but not all of the women seem to enjoy going to the woods to get their kindling, even though Redfield and others note that carrying wood is a man's job.

In Chan Kom life is divided in such a way that man and woman depend on each other for almost everything, an interdependence which is tied to subsistence living based on the corn culture. For life remains related to the corn god and the rain god, the two Mayan deities for whom ancient ceremonies are still held. In fact, according to local legend, God made the first people from corn.

The gods are still respected more than just worshipped. When I had to leave in a heavy thunderstorm, Doña Luz told me that *cha-chaac* (the god of water) did not want me to leave. "The *chac* is asking you to stay. It will be dangerous to go." There seemed to be no understanding of my reasons, which were such things as appointments or airline schedules. The villagers heard the *chac,* and knew I did not understand.

At the same time there is a great mixture of Mayan and Christian worship services. As Redfield noted, these people are "ceremonially as well as linguistically bilingual" (Redfield/Villa Rojas, 1934, p. 124). Many families have home altars to Fátima, Niña de Atocha, San Antonio. In some they are decorated with streamers and candles and embroidered dresses and altar cloths, and in others they are simple tables with a Mayan cross. Don Trini seemed a bit jealous of these home altars, saying that he felt God would want his work carried on in his "office," the church, not at people's homes. Some of the women seem extremely devoted to their saints, but also go out of their way to attend mass and to participate in church festivals.

In talking with both the men and women, I felt that the Mayan gods were, as they said, "Like the saints and apostles." They still perform ceremonies where, as Anita Brenner said so well, there are "idols behind altars" (Brenner, 1929, 1970). The *h-men* call on Mayan and Catholic persons, and the Mayan cross is in the altar of the church. They still hear the *chac* speak through thunder.

Certainly the expected responsibilities and activities of girls and boys are clearly related to corn. They are defined early during the *hetzmek* ceremony, a traditional Mayan ritual which is still performed in Chan Kom by most families. It is complete with godparents, *compadres* and *comadres,* just like baptismal ceremonies. The *hetzmek* takes place at the time the baby is first able to be carried astride the left hip. This is seen as a health precaution, since such spreading of the legs is supposed to make one strong and able to walk on long journeys. The ceremony is performed for girls when they are three months old, for boys when they are four months old. The difference was explained to me just as Morely reported it was explained to him in 1956 (Morely, 1956, p. 164): Symbolic of women's activities are the three stones of the hearth, and symbolic for men are the four corners of the cornfield.

I noticed the immediacy of the corn religion most in the daily ritual of tortilla making. As I was looking through the references to family life in Morely and Landa, I reread the detailed description of the making of tortillas.

1. The dried, shelled corn is first put into an *olla* or cooking pot, with sufficient water and lime to soften the kernels. The mixture is brought nearly to the boiling point and kept at this temperature until the hull is softened, being stirred occasionally. The *olla* is then set aside and allowed to stand until the following morning. This softened corn is called *kuum* in Maya.

2. Sometime the next morning, the *kuum* is washed until it is perfectly clean and free of hulls.

3. The *kumm* is then ground. In ancient times this was done by hand with stone grinders, but today hand-operated metal mills have generally replaced them. The ground corn, which is called *zacan* in Maya, is covered with a cloth and allowed to stand until later in the morning.

4. About an hour before the main meal of the day, a small round table about fifteen inches high called the *banqueta* is washed. This table always stands near the *koben* or typical Maya three-stone hearth. Next a round griddle *(xamach)* is also wiped clean, placed on the hearth, and allowed to heat. A section of plantain leaf *(u lee haas)*, roughly six inches square, is heated on the *xamach* until it becomes soft and pliant then it is placed on the *banqueta* with a pinch of ashes underneath to make it turn easily on the low table. After these preliminary preparations the Maya woman is ready to make her tortillas *(ush)*.

5. She pinches off a lump of *zacan* about the size of a hen's egg and places it on the piece of plantain leaf. The left hand forms the edge of the tortilla while the right flattens the lump of *zacan* and, at the same time, gives it a rotary motion on the *banqueta*. A round, thin, flat cake rapidly takes form under her fingers. The almost continuous pats produce a typical sound, heard through all Maya villages at midday (but very different from the sounds in other parts of Mexico of tortilla making). When shaped, the tortilla is laid on the heated *xamach* until it puffs out, when the woman picks it up and flattens it again with a blow on the table. Finally the tortilla is placed in a gourd *(lec)* to keep it hot; the average Maya man usually eats nearly twenty at one meal, and demands that they be piping hot.

(Morely, 1956, p. 175)

I noticed no difference from what I had just written in my own journal, step by step, except that the plantain leaf has been exchanged for a piece of plastic, and the hand grinder has been replaced by the

gasoline grist mill. Landa's sixteenth century account of the preparation of tortillas was very similar, and I loved his description in which
he said "they made good and healthful bread. . . execpt that they are
bad to eat when they are cold, and so Indian women take a great deal
of trouble making it twice a day" (Tozzer, 1941, p. 90-91, Landa,
1566). The rhythm and pattern has remained unchanged for at least
four hundred years, and who knows for how much longer than that?

During a recent ethnographic film workshop at Temple University
I saw a documentary movie of a Japanese tea ceremony. Even with its
more formalized and stylistic movements, it reminded me strangely of
the tortilla-making ceremony in the thatched huts of Chan Kom. There
is a pride of craftsmanship in producing a thin, round, elegant tortilla,
and there is a joy is sharing it with family and friends. Both the making
and consuming of tortillas are communal affairs. The women at
ceremonial occasions, both political and religious, as well as in daily
living, sit in large circles, chatting, laughing and making tortillas, following a ritual. In this sense I am not using Durkheim's clear cut
distinction between sacred (rites) and profane (technological) acts.
Rather I am using the UNESCO definition which states that "ritual—
like etiquette, is a formal mode of behavior recognized as correct, but
unlike the latter implies belief in the operation of supernatural agencies or forces" (UNESCO Social Science Dictionary, 1964, p. 607).

The women do not seem to consider this work drudgery, even
though often as many as seven hours each day are spent doing it. I
think this is what Fromm and Maccoby meant when they said that in
"some peasant societies work is meant to be spiritually satisfying"
(Fromm/Maccoby, 1970, p. 120). To live is to make *milpa*—to raise
corn—and to raise corn is to be related to the Mayan gods, the god of
corn and the god of rain. Farming and household labor are bound
together in religion; both man and woman feel the dignity of preparing
corn. The women love the *milpas* as well as the men, and feel a part
of the whole corn circle, from seed to tortilla. They often invited me
to go with them to help weed, and were very sad that I could not be
there to celebrate with them the gathering of the first ripened corn, to
drink the fresh *atole*. On my last night in Chan Kom I was extended
an invitation by one of Don Trini's sons. "Now that you have filmed
the life of the village, you should film the *cha-chaac.*"This was, I knew,
the most elaborate of their ritual ceremonies, the one to bring rain,
and one where according to Redfield, "the presence of women is out
of the question" (Redfield, 1934, p. 69). I replied by saying that I did
not think I would be allowed to be present, much less to film the

cha-chaac. "Do come back," he said. "Only the French (Musee de l'Homme) have filmed it and we would like you to as well. A film of our life here is not complete without the *cha-chaac* ceremony." Seen as a grey-haired foreigner, was I someone who could not contaminate a ceremony by my presence? No matter what the reason, I was surprised and honored to be invited, and, more importantly, was made once again aware of the circle of their lives, with corn as the center both for men and for women.

4

Ethos

*"The constellation of acquired drives or motivations which are
characteristic of a culture, plus the goals . . . toward which cultural
activities are directed or upon which high value is placed."*
(John Gillin, "Ethos and Cultural Aspects of Personality")

Often during my time in Chan Kom I came face to face with attitudes,
concepts, and experiential evidence which challenged not only prior
assumptions stemming from my own background, but even my previous observations of Mexican peasant societies. I found myself using
such terms as love, quality of life, freedom, joy, and harmony—terms
on a high level of abstraction, yet to me unavoidable in any description
of Mayan village life. Subsequently, it has become clear to me that each
of these terms has meaning beyond dictionary definition, both for the
people I was studying and for me, to a degree that specific note should
be made of it.

A few examples may illustrate the point. There was in Chan Kom
very little talk of love, few overt demonstrations between the sexes,
little observable evidence of a loving community. Yet in conversations,
and later in more subtle ways, I found a strong perception on the part
of the women of love as a collective concept, one which related to
living together, working together, being together. It was reflected in
the absence of hierarchies, of obvious status symbols, and of competitive, submissive relationships between husbands and wives. One of the
more remarkable phenomena I did observe was the absence of domestic strife, quarrels, and altercations. At first I thought I had only to wait.
But in fact not once in my several visits to Chan Kom did I witness
vicious, bitter, or violent behavior within the community.

One of the difficulties I have become continually more aware of in

analyzing the roles of Mayan women is that these women feel themselves to be a very real part of the mosaic of their community life. They
do not think of the men's part in the community as being more important than their own. As the women discussed their roles it was as if they
were reciting the "rules of the game," or perhaps the recipe for a good
rainfall or harvest: We prepare the food and take care of the chickens;
the men, they do this and that. The women were not competing or
comparing—they were just describing.

This cooperative feeling ties into the ethos of the enlarged family
group and that of the village itself. In their daily lives there are no
formal assignments of tasks, no "wheel" for chores as at the Lama
Foundation, a relatively successful intentional community based on
the principles of Eastern mysticism. There was no feeling of being
"relegated to the kitchen," as at New Buffalo, a community in New
Mexico, where female members finally walked out in protest *(Report
on Intentional Communities,* New College, 1971). The women are
very well informed concerning plans being made for Chan Kom—the
road, electricity, fiestas, etc. They are aware of their roles in a social
structure which would collapse without them. Everyone has a place, a
non competitive status which carries over to the male-female relationships. There is a harmony, in the Greek sense, a universality, a fitness
of things. This same feeling was described by Villa Rojas in his Journal
of 1931:

> A happy peace reigns hereabouts without hatred and without rancor, as
> if humanity through some unexpected miracle had suddenly turned good,
> thinking only of work. The women, in the shade of friendly trees, wash
> or wring out clothes, humming *jaranas* that they have heard in some
> *vaqueria;* the little boys give water to thirsty cattle that stand blandly near
> the *cenote,* or cut wood in the neighboring bush; while the men in the
> distant *milpas* care for the land which, punished often by the burning heat
> of the sun, grants no more than that which is indispensable for the ele-
> mental needs.
>
> (Redfield/Villa Rojas, 1934)

Even the absence of any dependence on alcohol seemed to confirm
this impression, since the loving atmosphere in work, play, and general
daily living gave every evidence of having removed the need for either
stimulants or depressants. In a conversation with Erich Fromm, he had
urged me to check on attitudes about alcoholism. I told him that Don
Trini had said on my first visit to Chan Kom, "There is no violence,
no alcoholism here. You can feel very safe here. If there is a drunk in
town he will be an outsider. Our only dangers are during fiestas, from
visitors." During my various trips to the village I encountered heavy

drinking only once, during the fiesta in November. I saw beer being sold only during one Sunday baseball game. Later I was told that beer was no longer sold. Why? "Because we know now that we have to have a license," said Amparo's husband, the storekeeper. But I wondered if there was more to it than that.

There is drinking during festivities, but rarely does it lead to drunkenness. As far as I know there are no alcoholics in Chan Kom. The ethos of a parity of roles in Chan Kom seem to fit well the model described by Fromm and Maccoby of a strong patriarchy, but with mutual respect between men and women to a degree that "there is no manifest war between the sexes, so that there is no reason for either sex to undermine the other; on the contrary both sexes feel relatively secure and hence *there is no need for escape into alcholism"* (Fromm/ Maccoby, 1970, p. 170). In their study of Las Cuevas, Fromm and Maccoby reported *that 48 percent of the men over forty were heavy drinkers or alcoholics (Ibid.,* p. 159). Unlike the abstainers in Las Cuevas who rejected "those activities which reinforce patterns of drinking" *(Ibid.,* p. 168), the people of Chan Kom refused to accept Protestantism with its restrictions against those very activities (fiestas, ritual ceremonies) which they valued, even though most, if not all, involve some use of alcohol.

In the Catholic Church itself, *atole* (a non-alcoholic drink made from corn) is served to the congregation by the women after the novenas. At the Fiesta of San Diego, the patron saint of Chan Kom, alcohol and beer were flowing freely on the plaza while the dance was being held in the town hall. According to the men, *balche* (the traditional ceremonial beer fermented with honey from the bark of the lonchocarpus tree) is still used in ceremonies to the various Mayan gods, as reported by both Landa in the sixteenth century and by Redfield and Villa Rojas in the thirties. Since these ceremonies are exclusively for men, I did not observe them, but I was invited to several other ceremonies where the *h-men* presided. The *h-men* discharges the function of both priest and shaman combining both the holy and the occult. Some form of alcohol—rum, anis, aguardiente—is an important part of many of these ceremonies. A small amount is passed ceremoniously around the group; the men and women seem to offer silent toasts to one another, and down it as if it were medicine. As the communal glass passes through the group, some people refuse it while others imbibe more freely, but it is the shaman who seems to be expected to reach a high state of intoxication as he calls on the saints and looks into his *aza-tun* (magic stone). I found it interesting that a part of the fee paid

to the *h-men* for this and also for his service as a medicine man is
alcohol. In fact the four bottles which he received were set up to
surround the table/altar, so they seemed to serve as something other
than merely payment (See Ana's vignette).

The gifts which are exchanged as part of the arranging of marriages
include rum along with such things as chocolate and cigarettes. However, Redfield reports that young men were refused as suitors if they
were known to drink (Redfield, 1950, p. 78). Continence is not seen
as a virtue in itself, but rather "drunkenness is wasteful" *(Ibid.,* p. 160).

In his journal of 1931, Villa Rojas noted that *"by general agreement
of the inhabitants* the sale of intoxicating liquors of any kind (was) not
permitted" (Redfield/Villa Rojas, 1934, p. 234).

Although Don Trini, predicted to Redfield that "the people would
become drunkards" after he and others of his generation die off, it
seems to me that the lack of alcohol use or dependence is more firmly
ingrained in the community-wide system of values which have been
discussed above.

This sense of harmony in the daily life of the community is further
illustrated by the interrelatedness of their agriculture with the Mayan
scheme of the religious cosmos:

> The agriculture of the Mayan Indians of southeastern Yucatan is not
> simply a way of securing food. It is also a way of worshipping the gods.
> Before a man plants, he builds an altar in the field and prays there . . .
> the cornfield . . . is a sort of temple. The cornfield is planted as an incident
> in a perpetual sacred contract between supernatural beings and men.
>   (Redfield and Warner, quoted in Lee, 1959, p. 166)

Although Redfield mentions only the men's roles in these ceremonies, I found the women, as mentioned above, to be proud of their
parts in them. There are, in fact, ceremonies from which men are
excluded such as the *meel Kanan Ha* (female guardians of the water),
in which the women among the Tzeltal Chiapas (highland Maya) par-
take in a ceremonial washing of the garments of the Catholic images
(Camara, 1966, p. 13). Many ethnographers omit these ceremonies
entirely or put them in a less important category than the people do
themselves.

In this text there are frequent references, both direct and indirect,
to the "quality" of life in Chan Kom, as perceived both by the residents
themselves and as observed by others. Of some importance, therefore,
is an understanding of what seem to be the characteristics of "the good
life" insofar as Chan Kom is concerned. The four attributes suggested
by Thomas and Znanieki (1958) in their study of Polish peasants seem
to fit rather closely the view held by those I talked with in Chan Kom.

They are: security, status, the desire to love and be loved, and a sense of curiosity. If one expands on these concepts, it becomes clear that there are rather especial meanings attached to each.

Security to the people of Chan Kom does not mean a sense of protection from cradle to grave as a result of accumulation of property or money. Rather, it reflects their recognition that most of the things they need or want are in fact ready at hand with a reasonable effort on their part. The result is that each feels his or her life is not fundamentally threatened, so long as normal rhythms are maintained and no new wants are created. The Aristotelian balance between desires and fulfillments has been maintained and is, in a way, even articulated, particularly in the general concern about the impact of the new road on their community. This expresses itself in the ambiguity they feel about "progress," both the hope for meeting some of the few unfulfilled wants they feel, and the fear that new wants will be created faster than their capacity to satisfy them without serious disruption to the life they know.

This sense of security, in turn, leads into the matter of status. Again, the feeling of being needed, or having a real role to play and of being a functional part of the life of the village, means that each person does in fact have a clearly defined relationship to all the others whether within the center of work, family, festivities, etc. Thus, husbands and wives share daily tasks without programming or schedules, aware that there is an interdependence between them which defines their status and contributes to their mutual satisfactions.

The need to love and be loved, as a working part of the definition of the good life, finds its fruition in many ways. I have referred in the discussion of Family and Home to some of these manifestations. To those remarks can be added my personal observation that the level of loving partnership was extraordinarily high. There was, for example, little evidence of the *machismo* complex; rather, I found that husbands and wives had quietly trusting relationships, few competitive feelings and marriages which, although they may already have lost some of the ceremonial and sacred aspects of the older culture, seem still to retain a high level of harmony.

The concept of curiosity as a factor in the good life demands some special attention. There is, in Chan Kom, great respect for knowledge. In fact, as Fernando Cámara recently remarked, they seem to want knowledge rather than learning. It is, for example, illuminating to note that several of the sons of Don Trini had earlier been offered opportunities for more schooling in Mérida, but that the decision had been

negative, reflecting an attitude not unlike that of the contemporary
Amish in the United States that too much learning could destroy the
integrity of the community. Nevertheless, there does exist a desire for
concrete information, for explanation and enlightenment about the
way things are. Although this apparent paradox occasionally caused
me some worry in trying to understand Chan Kom, further observation
and conversation confirmed a sense of consistency and harmony in the
people's own perception of their need for knowledge. They asked
questions about the outside world with openness and innocence, and
showed their appreciation for answers, even when it was quite apparent that they really lacked the learning to understand fully the nature
of the answers they received. William Herman notes that this perhaps
illustrates an ability to fit alien or strange ideas and information into
an orderly, sensible, and thus secure framework of a world view.

This sometimes confused "fitting" is nicely brought out in an entry
in Villa Rojas's journal, writing about the visit to the village of a
medical doctor:

> Last time that Dr. Shattuck was here he made a speech . . . on the cause
> of disease, saying that 'they are not caused by evil winds, but by microor-
> ganisms . . . that attack people in incalculable mumbers, if they are not
> prevented . . . ' He spoke with brilliant effect and brought it about that
> for quite a time everybody in the village was sick, since there was hardly
> a person who did not feel inside him strange ticklings, caused, it appeared,
> by the 'little ants' . . . that were consuming their vitals. This gave the
> *h-men* much business, in driving these noxious creatures out of their hosts
> by proper exorcisms.

> A similar disquietude was aroused when Dr. Sandground spoke on vita-
> mins. The tomato, previously so unappreciated, became for a few days an
> exquisite comestible. Perhaps now everything has returned to its normal
> state: the microbes have never existed and the vitamins are but the fanta-
> sies of wise men.

> (Redfield/Villa Rojas, 1934, p. 244)

Along with this feeling of wisdom in their own world the people of
Chan Kom have a respect for schooling, but just to the point where it
does not conflict with their own knowledge and their own lives. When
there were no more than twenty families in the village they built a
school there, in spite of tragedy and death involved in a construction
mishap. They struggled to obtain furniture for their own school so that
the children would not have to leave the village for their education.

But along with this curiosity, hunger for knowledge, interest in
learning new things, there is a respect for work, for diligence in,
Dorothy Lee's definition of the feelings of Greek peasants.

> Diligence is an internal attitude: it rests on self-discipline and free incentive, it includes interest and enjoyment. It does not mean a valuation of work for its own sake; it is the personal quality of diligence, not work itself, which is good . . .
>
> (Lee, 1959, p. 150)

As I lived in the village and talked with the women, I tried to decide how they felt about their long hours of work, particularly the extra hours of sewing and especially those hours at the sewing machines. Was it just for extra money, as Victoria had suggested? Was it compulsive, part of the Protestant ethic, as Redfield had suggested? For most of the women this just did not seem to be true. Work was explained to me as a need of man, not a necessity for man. When I was told "to work is to live," I was confused. But when I followed up with questions, I learned that the women of Chan Kom felt that work was like food, that one could become ill without work just as one could wither away without food. Another aspect of their attitude toward work was their evident difficulty in separating work from living, work from play or work from dignity. Work somehow seemed to be non-separated from being and non-separable from it. The Calvinist, Protestant, ethos concept of work as obligation or duty was simply not present. Rather work was talked about as creativity, as satisfaction.

In fact, Villa Rojas told me that the Mayan word for work, *meyah,* is nearer in meaning to the Spanish word *crear* (create) than *trabajar* (to work).

I realized I had misunderstood the concept of work in the village when I finally understood the use of the adjective *muy trabajadora* (hard working). Demetrio, in describing to me why he had chosen Anita for his future wife in spite of the need to wait three years until she became seventeen and old enough to marry, had said, "I could tell that Anita was *muy lista* (bright, alert, ready). She spoke good Spanish and was *muy trabajadora.*" I bristled at this remark since it seemed to me he only wanted someone to work for him. But later I saw this as meaning diligent—hard working as a part of basic personality. I understood. Anita is hard working, and misses her sewing machine, which she enjoyed. But in her work there is no feeling of hurry or compulsiveness. She always seems to be doing little things with her children— helping them learn songs, numbers, whatever—all with joy and a high level of personal involvement. She is *muy trabajadora.*

In trying to understand the concept of work in Chan Kom, I thought back to the Redfield-Villa Rojas quotation which is still often used: "To live is to make *milpa.*" This had been considered man's work by ethnographers, but now, and perhaps always in the eyes of the community, we can observe that it is not so limited. "To live is to work," and to work is to participate in a shared network of tasks for both men and women.

5

Progress

"Ninety per cent of all its achievements seem only to aim at alleviating the nuisance from the ten per cent which have a positive value."

(Levi-Strauss, 1972, p. 2)

Although I fully realize that Chan Kom cannot be considered typical, even of Mayan villages in Southern Yucatan, I do feel that some of the information and insights which resulted from this study may be of interest, and possible use, within the total context of available ethnographic and historical materials. The women interviewed were not chosen as a deliberate and representative sample, and in fact represent only a narrow group, all related to the single most dominant family in Chan Kom. Perhaps for this very reason however, it was possible to develop a rather special kind of familial and personal relationship with the whole group, which led to far more depth in the investigation than would have been possible had I selected a more scientifically valid sampling.

To understand the usefulness of the group with which I ultimately worked, it must be recognized that they do represent a cross-section of female roles in that they include all the major categories of age, marital status, and size of family. Thus, the intensity of the relationship and the variety within the limited framework of Chan Kom well compensate for the lack of a broader base, and have allowed my own role as activist-observer to develop naturally. As a result, I have come to observations and conclusions supported in depth by the people themselves, by my own closeness to the women, and by a wealth of background material accumulated over several centuries.

The most salient conclusion I have drawn from this study relates to change. Mayan women not only accept change, they will initiate and even agitate for change—even against the wishes of their husbands or the highly respected teachers—if it seems to be in the best interests of themselves or their children. Mayan women are not frightened by a new language, either literal or metaphorical, since they are already bi-lingual: linguistically, culturally and "ceremonially," as Redfield put it. They are strangely sophisticated peasants who have somehow absorbed from the Spanish culture what they want from it, without, in the process, losing much which they value from the traditional pre-Columbian culture, above all the corn culture. They appear not to have realized, or not to want to realize, that the old culture is passing, that matters beyond their control have made the old concept of "to make *milpa* is to live" an anachronism, perhaps even a myth. They still cling to the value system of the *milpa,* even while changing in many other ways. Parenthetically, it is interesting to note that as early as 1965 Goldkind questioned Redfield's widely accepted observations about the corn culture and the statement that all or most were subsistence farmers with equal income and status *(American Anthropologist,* 1965, V. 678, pp. 67-68).

The facts speak for themselves. Don Trini no longer cultivates his *milpa.* Of his six sons, only two made *milpa* last year, and of those two, one of them works part time as a traveling salesman-buyer and the other is rapidly bringing cattle to his private ranch and thus becoming less dependent on corn. In contrast, when we check on his daughters, we find that both of them in Chan Kom are still tied closely to the life of the *milpa.* The widow, Gabriela, works with her sons in the fields, and the only source of income for Marta and her husband Rufino is their earning from the corn they raise and from the produce and household animals they sell. Nonetheless, it was one of the *milpero* sons who invited, even urged me, to film the *Chac-Chaac* ceremony, if I was to get a complete film-record of the real life of the village. "It will be incomplete without it," he said. I wondered if he was not reflecting his vague subconscious feelings that there might not be many more such ceremonies, though I am sure he would never have admitted it.

But unless something drastic happens, I foresee the approaching end of the corn culture, and with it the relationship to the Mayan Gods and the *milpa* -based intertwining of the lives of the men and women. It may be that the family with whom I was living is in the process of repeating history (Strickon, 1965, pp. 46-47). They may be on the verge of returning to the combination cattle and maize culture in *hacienda* complexes which had been introduced by the Spaniards. This resulted in an extension of the pure corn agricultural patterns of the earliest Mayans without disturbing basic life patterns. The cattle ranches, in turn, were supplanted by huge sugar and henequen plantations. These "factories in the field," as Strickon called them, were highly destructive of village life and cultural patterns, and it was from them that many people fled to renew their traditional way of life. Many, in fact, fought for their old ways in the War of the Castes. Now again, the people of Chan Kom appear to be adding cattle as a source of income which is compatible with their ways of life and value systems. Today some of the young males, including two of Don Trini's sons, refer to themselves as *vaqueros* (cowboys) and their wives do so as well. Hopefully this new development will prevent *some* of the possible dehumanization effects which the new road forebodes and will help Chan Kom to avoid some of the problems of the consumer society.

I see the cattle and the increase in the production of handicrafts (and their sale) by women and children as supplements to the corn economy, as ways to increase their monetary wealth in order to purchase the medicines and other new commodities which they will desire without destroying present life styles. With these changes, corn will remain central as food for people and domestic animals, so perhaps the basic cultural patterns of the village will not be destroyed. Possibly even milk cows will be introduced, and better corn, although I have trouble picturing hybrid corn in the stony *milpas,* placed in the ground with a planting stick without the use of special feritlizers.

In the 1930s Don Trini pictured a Chan Kom millenium,

> when everyone will live in a masonry house and own cattle, and a phonograph, when a village cooperative will market fruit and corn by means of a collectively owned automobile (truck), when all necessary domestic industries will be performed in Chan Kom itself so that specialized labor will not have to be brought in from outside, when Chan Kom will be head of its own *municipio,* and when the Americans will drive to Chan Kom by automobile to admire and further dignify the paramount community of Yucatan. . .
>
> (Redfield, 1950, p. 34)

This statement is still largely a dream, and I should make it clear that Don Trini now experiences both hope for modernization and fear of it: I felt this ambivalence among the women as well. One of the fears that was often mentioned was pollution, smells, noise, and dirt as in the city. As I had looked around me on my first visit to Chan Kom, I had felt a strange feeling of being in a balanced aquarium. In the thatched hut where I ate and chatted, I never saw a fly, never even an ant. In spite of the setting turkey in the corner, the hens and chickens, the innumerable pigs and dogs in the yard, I never once stepped in filth—not even in the dark. Baby chickens ate the fleas off sleeping dogs. This strange cleanliness, this exciting ecological equilibrium, continued to amaze me everywhere until my last trip to Chan Kom. When the road opened, when the fiesta began, when the festive meals of chicken and pig began, when the outsiders started arriving, all at once there were swarms of flies—in the corner store, in my room, in the plaza. I saw three scorpions in one day. Perhaps it was simply coincidence, but I felt that the aquarium was already being thrown out of balance. But this original equilibrium was just a part of the larger feeling of harmony with nature, with earth and sky and wind and water, with the feeling that all essentials are really present. As Landa reports amusedly, even the dishes were provided by God. The Indians simply picked them from the trees, where God had provided them with *jícaras.* The women have a profound, perhaps organic sense of the wisdom of the world, and they share it with their children.

With the products of nature, the leaves, the fruits, nuts, flowers, bees—so valued for their honey that they have a special sacred place and ceremony—and the wild and domestic animals, all this combined with corn, life could be very complete. We have talked a great deal about tortillas, but should remember all the other corn-based foods: *atole, pozole, tamales, enchiladas.* In fact, this basic staple makes up to 85 percent of their diet. Corn is related as well to ceremonial occasions. *Atole* is served in its *jícara* at the church ceremonies for the dead *(finados),* and there is earth corn bread for the special services at the home altars.

The biggest handicap to modernization appears to consist of old beliefs and traditions deeply rooted in the Mayan character; non-pecuniary motives are illustrative. Avila, as Foster earlier, has noted that:

> Many times oppportunities for profit are foregone, either because there is a sentimental attachment to traditional ways, or because business and pleasure are not clearly separated, and the former does not necessarily take precedence over the latter . . . Moreover in Chan Kom 'wage earners' insisted on being paid in corn rather than in money, even though the corn was worth less than the money which would have been paid.
>
> (Alvila, 1969, p. 40)

He seems to forget that corn is a special commodity which carries with it a religious connotation as well as one of subsistence. We can go back to Stuart Chase's well known description of one of the characteristics of the peasant society.

The motive of the market as a whole is not a pecuniary one. People do not go to make a profit; they go to deliver what they have made and get what they need, and pass the time of day. The Aztec marriage of market day and holiday has never been dissolved.

(Avila, 1969, pp. 177-8)

Why must the marriage of market day and holiday be dissolved? Why must one go sell just to make a profit? The renaissance fair was able to combine business and pleasure; perhaps this is a positive attribute.

For the women, selling their products at home or at Chichen Itza is not only pleasure, a holiday, but also a chance to display a product, really an art show. Displaying of hammocks and embroidery is done with pride. Of course women want to sell, just as an artist would his paintings, but the money is not the sole reason. This feeling carries over into other products, whether made or raised.

One of the things which surprised me in Chan Kom as I talked with the women was the great emphasis on the monetary value of things. They are always asking about the cost of things, but I was never sure how much this was part of their curiosity about the outside world and how much had to do with actual cash value. Was this attitude a contradiction of the supposed lack of understanding of cash values or the profit motive? After observing and talking with the women, I felt that it was more than just crass monetary interest; this was part of their decidedly healthy curiosity. A genuine hunger for knowledge is demonstrated by trying to relate cash value to the outside world. They know poverty and want to have enough money to insure independence and security. But it is not just money they want; most of the women strongly desire to continue their learning. For example, I later had requests for English lessons from several of the women and children. They would ask for numbers and words, study, then come back and repeat them. Anita would write the numbers out phonetically in Spanish so they could be pronounced and learned by her children. They did this as a family game. They know Spanish and Maya; English is easy.

Another example of the way in which Mayan women desire to learn and accept change is their attitude toward birth control information. Far from being frightened or suspicious, they are eager to communicate and to trade, to try to come to terms with their new possibilities. The women feel that the new road is not so much a way to escape their village but rather a road *in,* a way to bring *prosperidad* to Chan Kom. Having access to medical care is a part of this prosperity.

At the same time, however, the women have seemed so far to resist change if the old way is preferred. They have in general, for example, retained the *huipul* in spite of pressures from the school teachers and from some husbands who feel that modern dress is *de más categoría* (more fashionable). And we have Redfield's thorough description of the events surrounding the short-lived "conversion" of most of the village to Protestantism during the late 1920s and early thirties. Some of the community, he says,

> were becoming sure that they could not accept the uncompromising Protestantism. . . They could not, and their women especially would not, give up all that becoming a Protestant required.
>
> (Redfield, 1950, p. 99)

There are probably many other things which will be retained or returned to. Determining what part the women will have in decision-making processes is difficult, particularly as they face new choices in the future. In fact, it is practically impossible to know who makes decisions at any time. My own feeling in Chan Kom was that family decisions are joint decisions, made only after mutual sharing of knowledge. I tend to agree with Villa Rojas' interpretation concerning the Yucatecan Mayan woman.

> The woman, although knowing the money received from the sale of eggs.
> . . is hers, thus prefers to have her husband's advice before she spends it.
> The same is true of the husband, in an important purchase, such as a cow or a horse.
>
> (Villa Rojas, 1969, p. 263)

Within the structure there is freedom and a searching for consensus.

Women in Chan Kom see the road as an enlarging potential for good life. They do not see it as an escape; but, one wonders, will they be able to resist the road out which has entrapped so many peasants by changing their lives from the rural, subsistence economy to the meager existence of the urban culture of poverty? These and other questions are real. One way out does lead to the pockets of poverty which compose the *barrios* and the soulless ghettos of the inner city, both in Latin America and the United States. In this move out, many experience culture shock, and too often the women suffer most.

The women leave a subsistence economy where they have been part of a mutually dependent relationship with their husbands for an urban ghetto where their role is undefined, uncertain, undignified, and rarely possible to redefine in a culturally meaningful way. Often there are fewer opportunities for employment, and those which seem tempting turn out to have much less status than the traditional roles in the village. Moreover, one crucially important role, that of the mother as map-builder and guide for the young, is lost. No longer is she connected to communications networks, half-hidden but very real, which work so well in the village. Admittedly the problem is a complex one, for at the other end of the scale:

> ... is the peasant community in which all work is essential for survival and thus all work has dignity. The man and woman exist in an interdependent relationship in which each has status, but neither is free to change.
>
> (Elmendorf, 1971, p. 18)

One of the questions I have often pondered is whether or not there is more joy or sorrow in the lives of the Mexican peasants, particularly in those of women, than is usually perceived. Was there less cruelty and suffering and more loving and enjoyment? I had always intuited this, and in Chan Kom I certainly found it to be so. During the mid-fifties, when Oscar Lewis was concentrating on the culture of poverty in Mexico, I tried to point out that I felt he was seeing only the negative traits of that culture. So it was particularly gratifying to find this observation from Lewis: "But when all is said and done, people in the culture of poverty are less lonely and less alienated than the modern middle-class man is" (Cited by Finney, 1969, p. 312). All my data substantiate the fact that the woman in Chan Kom is far less alienated than most of her sisters in the United States today.

One of the reasons I had wanted to go back to a traditional peasant society was to see if, as Fromm and Maccoby had suggested, there was a higher level of productiveness and a greater enjoyment of life than in the *mestizo* village which they had studied and with which I was also quite familiar. Again, as I have repeatedly observed, there does in fact appear to be a greater enjoyment of life among the Chan Kom women than had been observed in Las Cuevas, or in most *mestizo* villages, or for that matter, in most communities in the U.S.A. The women constantly display their sense of pride and pleasure in most aspects of their lives, conveying a feeling of dignity as well as pride. And, most importantly, there is a sense of harmony with each other, with nature, within their total world.

6

Summary and Conclusions

I had felt the power of an organic rhythm of life in Chan Kom during all but my last trip, when the excitement of the celebration of All Souls and All Saints, the Festival of San Diego, patron saint of the village, and completion and formal opening of the road, after forty years of effort, broke the peacefulness. Now there were firecrackers, dynamite, marching bands, chanting women, competing orchestras, singing, late night dances, early masses, bull fights, the *Pib,* the *gremios,* pigs dashing through the plaza, and just a general frenetic activity. Even the governor's arrival by helicopter to celebrate the opening of the road seemed only a part of the same keyed-up beat.

But while I resented the intrusion of noise and frenzied activity into Chan Kom, I began to see other new things, new interactions, new supportive patterns. Everyone was caught up in the importance and excitement of this biennial Fiesta. People whom I had never seen talk to each other on my previous visits were now preparing feasts together. Clothing was being bought to last for the next two years. The men were helping one another repaint the village in anticipation of the Governor's arrival. Five of them stayed up all night painting one house and a store by moonlight. The moon was full that night and it was time for the celebration of All Saints and All Souls. I had expected to see night-long vigils in the cemetery, but this activity seemed completely out of character with the village I had known. It was not simply the celebrations and the Fiesta. I wondered what this new road, anticipated for so long, was going to do to life in Chan Kom. What did these people, now my friends, want the road to bring them? Would they have a choice? I hoped that the road would bring them prosperity, but not at the price of the individuality of Chan Kom. In the immensity of the impending changes, would anyone have the time or opportunity to choose what things in his life he wanted altered, and what things to remain the same?

Two things representing potential change entered the village the first day the road was opened. The first was a large bright red truck from Mérida, loaded with cheap yard goods, household items, and odds and ends of things. The women were excited. The only material they had general access to before was the lovely white poplin which they use to make their *huipiles.* Only a few of the women in Chan Kom now wear dresses rather than the *huipil.* Would that start to change? Would the women gradually stop their "painting with needles"? I just did not know. The second thing was the arrival of the new school teachers, who came in chaperoned by their grandmothers. Not only were they among the first young women school teachers ever to come to Chan Kom, they were also the first women most of the villagers had ever seen in mini-skirts. When one of them would stroll across the plaza in pants and a sweat shirt, people simply stopped whatever they were doing and stared. What effect would these young women have on the women of Chan Kom, and on their daughters?

I wondered about my own role in all of this. When I arrived the women were reticent at first, but as confidence grew, they were eager to discuss countless things, with methods of birth control as one of the recurrent topics. Of the dozen who discussed this seriously with me, only the midwife who works as the priest's housekeeper claimed to oppose birth control on moral grounds. With a Mayan-speaking doctor taking over the nearby clinic, it seems only a matter of time before something is done. He is in favor of birth control, and was trained in various methods at a clinic in Mexico City. I have talked with him, and he is interested in setting up a branch of his clinic in Chan Kom. And of course, with the expected bus service now that the road is open, the women will be able to reach the regular clinic more easily.

The other point at which I felt I was interjecting myself into these people's lives, for better or for worse, came during the visit of the governor. Earlier that day, the women had been talking excitedly among themselves about how happy they would be when the tourists started coming, though none really could say why or what they were expecting. They all had plans, although daydreams might be a more accurate description for the tourists they expected. It occurred to me that tourists were probably the only hope for more income for Chan Kom. Listening to their dreams, I realized that the hope for tourists would be met only if Chan Kom had something special—a new Mayan ruin, or a *rústico* restaurant, perhaps by the *cenote.* But their *cenote* is not as big as the one in Valladolid, and has no history of hidden gold and sacrificed virgins like the one in Chichen Itza. But Chan Kom does have, I had recently learned, an exciting stretch of *sacbé* just two kilometers away. The National Geographic describes the *sacbé* as the longest extant Mayan highway—a beautiful, broad road, fifteen feet wide, raised high and built in a perfectly straight line through the jungle from Yaxuna to Coba, two well-known classic ruins. This intrigued me. Would it intrigue the thousands of tourists who visit Yucatan annually? After testing the idea out on the governor's assistant, I sat down behind the table where the governor was eating breakfast and asked him if he knew that the *sacbé* was less than two miles away. The governor checked me carefully, asking specific questions. I quoted my sources and told him about the maps I had checked, and that the people of Chan Kom had informed me that the road from the plaza goes right to the *sacbé,* but is not passable for cars. Without hesitation the governor rose.

I just had a great idea.

And he turned back to thank me.

> I'm going to talk immediately to the Department of Public Works and ask that the road from Chan Kom be extended to the ancient *sacbé* built by our Mayan ancestors, from the great ceremonial center at Coba. Then the brush can be cleared away, and through Chan Kom people can reach a previously isolated area of Yucatan. And people from the *rancherias* and *milpas* along the way will be able to come into Chan Kom. While the caterpillar and heavy machinery and men are here, I would like to see the highway extended two kilometers more. I am going to push this personally. You have my word.

Don Trinidad stood immediately and translated his words into Mayan. Everyone applauded, and Alvaro, the *presidente municipal* who had done much to bring in the road, looked delighted. Then the governor's party made a tour of the plaza, and left in their helicopter. As they were passing out of sight, the great yellow caterpillar arrived on the plaza. It was the first time the women and children had seen the huge machinery used on the road, so there was great excitement. I wondered for a moment if it was going to start building the road to the *sacbé,* but I knew it couldn't be true. Instead, the caterpillar climbed the little hill and destroyed the strangely beautiful, Greek-like open air theatre while people watched and applauded. "Why?" I asked. "The governor ordered it, Señora. We don't need it now. There will be a *cine* (movie theatre) soon, and electricity for the *cenote*—everything. Chan Kom will be an important village. We are civilized now."

I heard this sadly but without surprise. The people had loved that theatre with its occasional plays and poetry readings. It had been an integral part of their lives. Now, at a word from the governor it was gone. How many other things would be senselessly sacrificed for a "progress" which no one was sure benefitted even the most "civilized" of nations? I wondered about the tourists and the *sacbé* and Chan Kom. I had not wanted to manipulate anything, but then I could not remain a passive observer, holding back information which might help the village. Were the tourists going to be more polluting than helpful? I just did not know. If they came to visit the *sacbé*—a monument to the skill and ingenuity of the ancient Mayans—would the tourists somehow share in the sense of this heritage? And would this somehow cause less of a loss of pride in the past and respect for their own way of life in Chan Kom? I wished I could be sure.

I left the village the last time with ambivalent feelings. From the huge coca-cola advertisement painted on the multi-colored store, once all white, to the mini-skirted school teachers, it was obvious that Chan Kom was turning away from its past and beginning a new stage of existence. Would the men and women remain contented with their lives, each believing the other's job to be more difficult? Or would the exposure that the road might bring make them feel "backward," "underdeveloped," and soon discontent to live the lives in which they once had such joy and pride? Would the road bring in the many benefits of modernization, or would the changes overwhelm them, sending those still able to leave back up into the peaceful bush country? Would the women have any part in making the choices that would affect their lives, as many had before, would they see their roles as women and as mothers particularly minimized as they came into contact with a civilization to which their past experience did not relate?

Afterword 1

It is my hope that this study has furnished some new information, new insights into the cross-cultural study of women, new knowledge of Chan Kom, and perhaps shed new light on the impacts of "progress" and "traditionalism." In many ways, however, much of the value of the experience of learning for me was in the mutuality of the process. All along the way I was concerned lest I be guilty of "cultural pollution," a major sin to me and one which I had too often observed in other settings. I had my hang-ups about the possible effect of my presence alone, yet I kept coming back to Freire's statement: "Dialogue, as the encounter among men to 'name' the world, is a fundamental precondition for their true humanization" (Freire, 1971, p. 133). Certainly I did not want to impose an ideology or prove a theory—both forms of cultural oppression—but rather I hoped that the book I might produce (and the film which would accompany it) would help increase understanding and self-identification on the part of the women of Chan Kom.

The process of mutual learning was a creative pact. We shared hopes, fears, and knowledge as they faced the challenge of all the change the road might bring in and take out. I tried to learn about their world, its meanings and its values. The women's new understanding of birth control techniques and their search for control of their biological destiny is exciting, both to them and to me. This was but one of many insights which lent validity to Jacobs' observation that, "at this point, we cannot say for certain that women in groups do what men . . . say they do, nor do women necessarily conceive of themselves and their world in the way men report these findings" (1971, p. 3). Perhaps as a woman talking with the women of Chan Kom, I was able to both feel and observe their problems in a way which a man might not have. I found a dual problem: to "humanize" their lives for other people by supplying some long-overdue ethnographic information on women; and to prevent in some way their "de-humanization" by the "progress," symbolized by the coming of the road.

This is an epilogue in a very specific sense, for I did make another visit to Chan Kom *after* the road had actually been opened and after the *sacbé* had been made accessible by a continuation of that road. Some of the hopes and fears we discussed earlier were then beginning to assume reality. There were in fact a few tourists beginning to appear and people were coming from the *rancherías* in greater numbers to make their purchases in Chan Kom. There was daily bus service out to Mérida and Valladolid and even to the *sacbé,* opening up completely new vistas of space, markets, and contact with the outside world. Yet the women could not believe that I hadn't somehow known about all this change. They did not understand why I had not come to the opening ceremonies, presided over by the Governor, despite the obvious fact that I had not had no word of it, no letter, no communication from them at all. "But," they said, "the *anunciador* birds told us you were coming. After all, the *sacbé* is your *sacbé,* too." In a way, I still felt some remorse at perhaps having helped open the doors of Chan Kom to a consumer society, or at the very least to the possibility of more tourism with everything that implies; they were clearly more concerned with the mysterious breakdown in telepathic communication between Florida and Yucatan.

Nonetheless, they were becoming more realistic about their plans and expectations. They were beginning to realize that there were *not* hordes of people waiting at the other end of the road just to come into Chan Kom; their talk of how many hotels and how many rooms would be needed was revised. In talking together of present realities, we began thinking of restaurants and small shops where their handicrafts could be displayed and sold. "Maybe we can have a cooperative here," the women said. From the idea of "fancy" restaurants—generated, perhaps, by the spectacle of Don Trini returning from Valladolid with the supplies for *his* restaurant, including gold-rimmed tumblers, plastic plates and flowered oil-cloth—we went on to talking about and planning typical Mayan settings, even joking about a sales promotion gimmick: "Eat with a Mayan family." There was imagination and good humor about all these prospects, but there was also a feeling on my part that technology, consumerism and Western entrepreneurship patterns were intruding into this peasant society, that the potential for their becoming "marginal people" was all too imminent.

But behind these fears and concerns, I kept returning to my own great faith in the humanity of these peasant women. I recalled a conversation with John Whiting, in which he commented on the peasant woman's relationship to change, observing emphatically that the controlling factor in their receptivity to new elements in their life is the effect that they may have on their children. He listed participation in family planning, education and the economy as being determined by specific considerations of whether they would result in a better life—not for themselves, but for their children. My mind went back to Redfield's statement:

> In every part of the world, generally speaking, peasantry have been a conservative factor in social change, a brake on revolution, a check on that disintegration of local society which often comes with rapid technological change.
>
> (Redfield, 1956, p. 137)

Beyond that, I consoled myself with the well-recognized fact that it is usually the women who are the conservers among the conservatives, the ones who try to hold on to the values, traditions and life styles they have learned to appreciate.

There are, I know, many warnings about the impact of modernization on peasant societies, some of them posing specific threats to the lives of women. Ester Boserup has stated: "Always there is the unfortunate result of enhancing the prestige of men and lowering the status of women. It is the men who do the modern things . . . as the developed countries share their techniques with the developing" (Boserup, 1971, p. 56). As I conclude this study however, my own optimism remains unabated. The harmony between the men and women of Chan Kom is deeply rooted. The sharing of daily tasks and the level of mutual respect I observed in almost every aspect of their living seem to provide a strong protective shield against the threats of a dehumanizing society outside their world. It may well be that the role of the women of Chan Kom, their creative participation in the life of community, is one rare example of a rich and deep-seated orientation to the real world which is strong enough to maintain its creativity, even in face of modernization and change.

Afterword 2

I arrived in Chan Kom this afternoon to check on my final data for the book manuscript, to take a few pictures for the new edition, and most importantly, to see how everyone is and what has happened since my last visit in March 1973.

As I drove into the city I was once again amazed at the beauty of the plaza, the careful planning which had gone into changing open space into planned space. Thatched roofs had been put on top of the new masonry buildings, and I was delighted to see that a thatched hut had been put up on the monument replacing the original little theater. Trees had grown around the *cenote,* children were playing on the swings, and a basketball game was underway in front of the office of the *presidente municipal.*

Balerio waved to me as I turned the corner in front of his store and stopped in front of Luz's house. Flora's children ran to meet me, and I was pulled into the kitchen of the thatched hut where Luz was clearing up after the noon meal. She wanted me to sit down and have something to eat, but I assured her I was not hungry and would prefer to make a little circle and say hello to everyone.

Next door at Anita's the doors were closed. One of the smallest children told me she was at home, but the older children insisted that she had gone out to her *solar.* I went on to Victoria's house. She was sitting, as she is nearly always sitting, at the sewing machine close to the doorway, and Alvaro was chatting with her as he sat on the bench at the back of the large room. Both of them looked much more relaxed than they had the last time I saw them. The strain of being the *presidente municipal* was over, and Alvaro was obviously relieved. He was in a reminiscing mood, and told me of his last visit with the governor when he had presented a list of the twenty accomplishments which had been carried out by the *ayuntamiento* (town fathers) and the *gente del pueblo* (people of the village) during his three years in office. The only copy of this list was then in the governor's office, but I asked Alvaro to remember as many of the projects as he could for my records.

Alvaro explained first that the projects had been made possible by the 25,000 pesos which comprised the town budget during his years in office. The money came from taxes on corn and fines for *delitos* (crimes) such as pig stealing, drunkardness, wife-beating, and so on. I asked more about wife-beating since I had heard so little about it during my stay in Chan Kom. Alvaro said that it was infrequent, and that the fines were levied according to the number and strength of the *golpes* (blows).

Although according to Alfonso Villa Rojas the concept of *fagina* (public labor) has practically disappeared, Alvaro told me that every family in town contributed its part to the projects, either with labor or with money. The materials and payment for the rest of the labor came out of the treasury. Federal and state funds were used in part for the more expensive projects such as the park, the monument, and the highway.

The first three projects Alvaro mentioned were the completion of the highway, the construction of the monument to its completion, and the planning and planting of the public park. This last is a truly beautiful example of what a town plaza can be: a useful center for community life, arranged for both play and rest, conversation and contemplation.

The installation of the drinking water was next, and the piping of the water to different sections of the town. (The water tank now towers above the school building.) A sports field was cleared at the edge of town, and although this is not used very much right now, Alvaro hopes that in time it will become more popular. With the remaining money in the treasury, an interesting combination of two other projects was finished. Seven meters were added to the church so that there would be less crowding, and a new *plaza de toros* was built. The money was divided equally between the two projects.

The next project was a *chiqueros,* the construction of a place to exhibit high quality pigs. A sidewalk was built in front of the school, the benches inside the school were painted, and roads were extended to various parts of town. Another project, which is being carried out with the help of the National Indian Institute, is the building of an irrigation system. This includes drilling a new well and building a reservoir, all with the cooperation of the townspeople.

Alvaro was obviously pleased with the accomplishments of his administration, but relieved to be finished with his term in office. The

people had wanted him to stay for another term, he explained, but he
didn't feel that he could, and was very happy to be back at his ranch.
Apparently it had been difficult to find a successor who had the time
and who really cared about Chan Kom, but finally Esteban, Marta's
husband, had agreed to take over. There was no opposing candidate.
As for the town council, the new members were elected for only two
years; their term of office will expire when the governor's does. (There
is, incidentally, no longer a woman on the town council as Berta's term
of office expired.)

Alvaro feels that one of the most important things he had done to
insure that Chan Kom would continue to progress was to turn down
all requests for a *cantina* license. He had four such requests during his
term, two from residents and two from outsiders. Alvaro feels that the
sale of alcohol, even beer, in Chan Kom would interfere with its progress. One of the requests for a license came from his brother Eduardo
and another from Máximo Huicap, a friend, both of whom were very
upset not to have received permission. It seems that *aguardiente* is still
sold clandestinely, but Alvaro believes that this is better than allowing
a *cantina* to open. "There is very little use of alcohol now in Chan
Kom," he explained, "and never while I live will there be a *cantina* in
Chan Kom. That would hold back the progress of Chan Kom and
progress for Chan Kom is what I want."

As we were talking, two young Mayan women walked in dressed in
beautifully embroidered *huipiles.* Each wore several golden chains; the
younger had a half permanent, although her black hair was pulled back
with a pink ribbon; the older woman's hair was severely pulled back
but she was also carefully groomed. Victoria explained that they came
from the *rancheria* of Xtoil, one in Chan Kom's municipality. They had
just come back from taking food to their husband who was in jail there.
"Their husband?" I asked.

Victoria laughed and explained that the older woman was the "real
wife" *(casada por civil).* "The young girl's father brought the man in
and asked that he be put in jail. The new *presidente Municipal* asked
us to take care of the young woman. Then the other wife, the married
one, came here too and asked to stay. So they are both here. They are
good friends. The man did not capture the young one. She wanted to
live with him. They went away together for eight days, and when they
came back the wife welcomed them both. The young one's father gave
her a good beating. She couldn't live at home. Her father is asking for
5,000 pesos and the trial is today. These women walked over two
leagues to get here and explain how things were. The real wife left

their two children at home. They visit the man together, cook his meals here. They haven't quarreled yet!"

Both Victoria and Alvaro seemed very confused by the situation, and there was much speculation as to the outcome of the trial. According to Victoria, the father is asking for 5,000 pesos because the man stole the affection of the girl. Alfonso Villa Rojas later observed that supposedly this was to remove the stain on the family's honor *(limpiar la mancha)*, but he could not believe that a price of money was being placed on such a thing.

During my visit with Don Trinidad I learned that he had been reading in all of his books to see what kind of advice he could give, as never before had he come across a case where a man had two wives who both seemed to be happy living with him. He explained, "Women have the right to vote at eighteen and they have the same rights as men, so I don't know whether or not they can choose to live together with a single man. I understand this is done in some countries by some people."

I asked how he felt this compared to the situation which he had found himself in, according to his autobiography, when he brought Luz to live with him.

He smiled wryly. "That was very different," he said. "As you might remember, my wife and her mother were the ones who disapproved of the situation. In this case the two women seem to be happy. And besides, why should the father get the 5,000 pesos?"

Back in Luz's kitchen, all the children of Anita, Flora and Gabriela crowded around, but I didn't see Ana or Armando. Luz explained that Ana's father had died. He had been in the hospital for a while; she didn't know what he had but he was very ill for a long time. (Luz looked quite tired to me, and her left eye is getting much cloudier.) She informed me that Ana and Jorge had moved back with them, and that she and Ana were cooking in the same kitchen.

"I wondered when I came in why the *nixtamal* was in the shed behind my first room here."

"Yes, they are living here now. The chauffeur and his family are living in their house. I don't know why."

Don Trini explained eventually that the chauffeur had been offered several places to stay, but he had turned them down and wanted either Don Trini's new store or Jorge's house. Don Trini was not willing to give up his store, so it was decided that Jorge and Ana would have to move out. When I asked if it wouldn't have been easier for him to give up the store he evaded the question.

"What about Ana's garden and her animals?"

"She goes every third day to water the garden. The señora is very nice."

The next morning I talked with Jorge and asked how he felt about it. He said that Ana had been very nervous after her father's death, and was alone a good deal since Armando was in school. He said he felt better with more people around her for a while. "She was getting very strange, Señora. After her father's death when she was alone for many hours, she would think her father was coming back to see her. I was worried. I think she's getting better now that she is with more people, though."

As always, I needed more time than I had to find out the true story. Ana did seem tense and I regretted that I had only a few minutes to spend with her. She did say that she had agreed to rent the house only for six months, and hoped that perhaps before that they could go finish an addition to the house and live in it. She understood how important it was for Chan Kom to have the chauffeur stay in town, and besides, he has really done a lot to improve the house. He painted the walls, fixed the floor, and the whole house seems nicer than it was.

I came by that Monday to find that Ana had spent the weekend with her mother who was still very much in mourning. Jorge had been in Piste with the band for a fiesta. On the corner table the band instruments were piled up, and I learned that Ana and Jorge and Armando were sleeping up in one of the vacant rooms in Victoria's house. So the wife of the family who had seemed the proudest of her house and of housekeeping had somehow changed completely. The *nixtamal* which she had run with such ease was now managed by Antonio's oldest daughter, and her hammock frame was stretched in an empty room in Victoria's house. I could still picture Ana in her old thatched hut with each needle just at fingertip. I wondered what had become of the kerosene stove which she was just trying out during my last visit. But this was the beginning of a new period for both of us, and there was no time for such questions.

I had brought a copy of Ana and Jorge's wedding picture which I had printed for them "in a lighter color" at their request. Both were delighted to see the results.

I had gone to see Marta before stopping at Ana's house, and learned that she had been very pleased by the book. She and her daughters read it carefully, and Marta said, "Yes, the book is fine with me. I have nothing I want you to change, but I would like to ask you to write another book, a book just for women about *la vida sexual* (sex life) to teach women how to keep from having too many children. My daugh-

ters each have too many children now, and I don't want them to have
any more. They don't want any, but my daughter Concepion is pregnant again." Concepcion was lying on the floor of the thatched hut,
having a massage by the *comadrona* at whose home I had attended a
wedding in the summer of 1973. They both asked me if I would take
them and Concepcion to meet the doctor in Xochenpich. This to me
took priority over the other things I had planned for Monday morning,
even over attending the trial which hadn't yet begun because the father
had not appeared. So I agreed to take them over to the clinic, if only
to meet the nurse in case the doctor wasn't there. Within less than half
an hour we had everything planned for a quick trip, and I drove over
to Xochenpich with Marta, Concepcion, her husband, Mariano Canah
Pech, the midwife, and the two-year-old daughter. As I had feared the
doctor was not there, but they had an opportunity to meet the nurse
who speaks perfect Mayan. She gave Concepcion a preliminary investigation and made an appointment for her with the doctor. When asked
about family planning information, the nurse gave them a booklet on
birth control prepared by the clinic; Marta invited the nurse and doctor
to come to Chan Kom and talk about setting up an extension clinic
there. The nurse then explained that a branch of the clinic would soon
be opened in Piste which was much more accessible to the people of
Chan Kom. In an emergency there would be transportation from the
clinic in Piste to the hospital in Xochenpich. On returning to Chan
Kom we were met by Marta's husband, Esteban, who was delighted to
hear that Concepcion was alright. I do not know what the follow-up
will be, but the first link in the network has been formed.

My last impressions of Chan Kom are a mixture of new and old faces,
and curiosity about some missing ones. Gabriela's two youngest
daughters have gone to Quintana Roo and are working together in a
tortilleria owned by an older daughter. Felicia had gone to spend New
Year's in Mérida with her aunt and had not come back yet. Antonio was
still working by the day, as Flora told me. Their little baby girl has
grown into a rather weakly child. She is Chela's responsibility, but
Chela didn't seem to show her much warmth and calls her *"Niña"*
rather than her name, Maria del Carmen. Chan Kom has a new woman
schoolteacher and also a new male teacher, José Pat. He is the nephew
of one of the founding fathers of Chan Kom, and as far as I know, one
of the first young Pat's to move back since the religious disturbance.

One familiar picture was that of Don Trini having coffee with the
new mayor Esteban. This had often been his habit when Alvaro was
in office. "I am giving him *consejo* (advice)." They were both very

concerned at the time about the law suit involving the man and the two wives. Esteban explained, "This is my first case. I have left my *milpa* this year for the first time—my sons will take care of it for me. I am going to dedicate myself to justice *("dedicarme a la justicia")."* He seemed to share much of Don Trini's sense of purpose for Chan Kom. Don Trini told me, "I have all the laws of Mexico and the laws of Chan Kom in my head. And when I don't know something I can check it in my books to be sure. But I haven't found anything yet about the case of the two women."

Afterword 3

On my way to Mexico for the seminar on Feminine Perspectives in Social Science Research in Latin America, I planned a stop in Yucatan so that I could go to Chan Kom and see what had happened in the six months since my last visit.

Everything looked green and damp as I drove through the outskirts of Merida, except for the henequen fields which looked sad as always. After a stop in Chichen Itza to freshen up and eat a taco, I hurried on to Chan Kom, eager to see what changes had come. I had continued being concerned about not having seen Anita on my last trip. Instead of stopping at Don Trini's house, as I always had done, I kept on to Anita's door. I stopped the car and was surrounded by her children. The door was open and there was Anita, waving from the kitchen. Out she came, smiling, and gave me a warm hug. I asked about the family.

"Everyone is well except my father, who is sick, very sick."

I knew how close she was to her father.

"What about going over to Muchucux-cah? How's the road, better than last time?"

She laughed with memories of having to turn around, of the dynamite, the rain.

"No problems now, can we really go?"

"I have no other plans, we can go early and come back before dark. Where is Demetrio?"

"Baking French bread with Lalo."

"Like old times," I said, remembering that Redfield had written of this and they had told me too. But I wondered why Amparo had given up her profession—I'd have to find out.

"I will go to saludar Dona Luz and then come back to see if you can go to Muchucux-cah."

"She's very ill, hasn't even been able to go to the pibs, not even leave

140

her hammock."

In the car I repeated the story of the last visit, how sorry I was not to have seen her, how much sorrier to feel that she had locked her door and pretended to be in the milpa. She interrupted:

"But I was in the milpa, really I was. I was sorry not to have seen you."

Then we started talking about the book, and I asked if there were parts she now wished weren't in the Spanish edition.

"No, I wouldn't have any part of my story changed, but I wish the young boys didn't just read part of it and tease the young girls, like Rosa and Felicia. If just we women had the book, like in the beginning —but now they have them to sell, and even with the names changed everyone knows who's who. Its just the young men. They turn it all around. But its the verdad, the truth, and I wouldn't want it changed."

But then she remembered the locked door.

"Who said I didn't want to see you?"

"Ana."

"I don't know why Ana would want to say that, but then Ana. . . "

And I didn't understand, but I was relieved to know I hadn't misused a confidence. But why had Ana said what she had said? But then there had always been this strained relationship between Anita and the others. What was it? Was it because she was from another village? A second wife? Grand-daughter of a shaman? Was it because of her greater reading ability? Singing ability? Or was it partly a personal jealousy of her friendship with me? As Beverly Chinas (1973, p. 112) noted, Zapotec women rarely express jealousy toward other women over men—whereas mestizas do—but they do express jealousy of women's friendship with other women. One of my most difficult tasks had been to maintain an open network of friends, trying always to divide my time, to be aware and concerned. I will never really know what happened unless I ask the children, but I didn't want to involve them in this.

Later with Alvaro we talked of many things, including our regular continuing discussion about pigmies. My card from Africa with the picture of the SS Universe campus hadn't arrived, but we spent a long time in the hut by the kitchen hearth talking about all kinds of Africans —Bushmen and Ibo and Masai and other peoples. What a delightful mind—so curious, so open.

And then he said, "The Minister of Education sent me four copies of the book, and I kept one for myself, and have read it carefully now. I am so glad you put in the part about the sacbe and the governor. That is just the way it was, and it has been so good for Chan Kom that the road went on and didn't just stop here. That was important. New communities are joining our town. Muchucux-cah has left Tekom and joined us. New families are moving into the edge of town and building their homes—some have come from nine leagues away. Many of our young people are leaving but new people are coming."

So I asked Alvaro about the book, about how some people felt it had been embarrassing to a few individuals, especially the women, about how I had put in the good and the bad.

"I wouldn't have changed any part, it is the truth, the reality of when you were here. It is no longer true because there have been changes already—many changes, but it caught Chan Kom at an important time, before the road came. Now there needs to be a new history. Are you writing another book? Are you going to write about the changes?"

"I am not planning to, in fact I had no idea of writing a book when I came to Chan Kom three years ago. I came to try to understand how your way of life . . . how you had maintained certain values and customs in spite of choosing progress. Of course, as you know, I was interested in knowing the parts the women had played in all this. You have taught me many things. I was surprised when the Ministry of Education wanted to publish it. Alfonso Villa Rojas told me that one of the main reasons was that it gave a picture of dignity and pride in village life—to Mayan village life—which many people would enjoy learning about, as did I. Also I want you in the village to know that the book was not a money-making project for me. I have gained a lot but in other ways."

"But we need another book, one to tell what's happening now—won't you do it?"

"Maybe Professor Villa will come back and do a fifty year summary, since he first came as your teacher—your maestro years ago. He says he would like to, maybe he will."

We continued talking about Chan Kom, about the new projects, the experimental farm organized by the National Indian Institute.

"It's a sociedad. We want to be a cooperative so everyone will learn how to raise and use tomatoes and melons and other things. It is good. But very little is happening in the mayor's office—he doesn't seem to know how."

"But then this is his first time," I said, "and after all it was your third and who could do as much as you did?"

We talked about Santa Rosa, his ranch, on the old road to Chichen, and on my way out I gave a lift to Alvaro and the two "hijos regaldos", who were listening to everything but saying little, and dropped them

off at the path through the brush to his ranch. "Next time you come
we'll have this cleared so you can come to Santa Rosa . . . Hasta
Luego."

The real part of my visit with Felicia started as we drove together to
Merida. Her father, Lalo had said when I picked her up with her five
year old brother-chaperone at the store:

"She can go with you this time, but don't steal her."

"You need her, don't you? I'll take care," and we smiled at each
other.

Felicia looked trim and fresh in a blue cotton dress with a sailor
collar, and ready for the city with her overnight bag and purse.

Just before getting into the VW, she made a list with her father of
supplies needed for the store so she could purchase them in the city.
Her list was carefully made, and her composure was amazing. It was
our first time alone since the trip to Xanla to see the robbed tomb.
Ostensibly she was going to see the doctor because she had a very bad
stomach upset, but she seemed in good health to me. As soon as Alvaro
and the boys got out she changed to the front seat with me and left
her little brother in the back—in such awe and wonder at this unex-
pected excursion that he stood looking out the window until he fell
back, sound asleep. We talked without stopping the two hours in to the
city.

First I asked about the family.

"Mother doesn't feel too well, she says her lungs hurt. With the new
baby and all, there is lots of work. "Did she have any difficulty with the
birth?"

"No, Dona Concepcion helped, and everything went smoothly."

"Tell her I was sorry not to have seen her. I heard she was in
Valladolid."

"She has been very sick, and very sad, since her favorite daughter
died . . . the one you knew. Remember the handwashing ceremony two
years ago—she was Dona Concepcion's youngest daughter and they
were very close. She died in childbirth with her mother helping. And
you know that Dona Concepcion had never lost a mother—and then
for it to be her own daughter. She just lived three hours after giving
birth to twins, and the twins died too, and her poor husband couldn't
believe it. People had to hold him. He knew she was calling him. And
he is left with the two little girls. They are staying with Dona Concepcion. No one knows what he will do. He is very fine, but very sad. You
know they had lost a baby earlier . . ."

We were both quiet for a long while.

She started then with questions about my family, mostly about my husband, who had been there only briefly, but who, to the people of Chan Kom was very real. The women especially wondered what kind of man would allow his wife to spend so much time in the field, travelling alone, driving alone—somehow the most daring of things. I explained that he had left for California for some meetings at the same time I had left for Merida and that we would meet in Mexico later in the month.

"But he trusts you so and you trust him. Has it always been that way? Is it that way with all couples in the USA? How do you find a man like that, how do you know ahead that a man is really like that?"

Hard questions to answer, but we talked about them in detail and then I asked about the cousin who had run away from Chan Kom the week the road opened, just before her wedding.

A laugh from Felicia.

"She is still in Merida, living with my sisters and working. She is happy. But guess what her ex-novio did. He married a girl from a rancheria, a girl who doesn't even speak Spanish. His mother says he can trust her; she will know what to do. She is glad that she didn't stay and marry him because neither he nor his mother trusted her or would let her do anything. She wasn't free. But guess what another boy from Chan Kom did; he married a mestiza and they are living in Merida. What do you think of that? Do you have mixed marriages in the states? Do you think its bad?"

I explained that that was a hard question to answer, that years ago when I got married I was from the south, my husband from the north, he one religion and I another, he with a German name and I a Scottish and that was considered "mixed" then. But then there are other mixed marriages between more different peoples, say Blacks and Whites, or Chinese/English, or Mexican/Anglo or Native American, and that some were happy couples and others weren't. My feeling was that marriage was a very personal thing which had to do with mutual respect and not with color, class or anything else . . . a contract between two people . . . and then *I* caught my breath. The conscientizacion of another, the opening of choices, is a great responsibility. Surely I wasn't going to kidnap Felicia, but had I stolen her?

Back to Chan Kom.

"Do you have a special boyfriend now, someone special?"

"There are several who are interested, but *todavia,* not yet. I'm not ready. How do you know about men ahead?"

And Felicia, who is twenty and getting old, told me about couples in the city and in the village who lived together and pretended to be married.

"Wouldn't you like to do that, to know a man first?"

"No, but I would like to be sure, and I don't yet know what I want to do. I wanted so much to go to Merida and now my two younger sisters are there. And Adelina, you remember, who didn't like to work in the store, she is in Quintana Roo, working in the tortilleria, run by my uncle, working with Dona Gabriela's girls. They only get two hundred pesos a month there, but they are with all their cousins and they like it. Its different. I like Merida better. Did you know that fifty people, eighteen girls, have left Chan Kom to work in Can Cum (the thriving new development touted as the Acapulco of the Caribbean). The girls are getting four hundred a month as kitchen helpers, most of them. And the men, like Antonio, are earning seven to eight hundred pesos a month. And with the road they, the men that is, get rides and come home on Saturdays and go back on Sundays, but the girls have to work on Sundays—weekends are the busiest times. They earn more money, but the ones in Merida, like my sisters and cousins, have a better time, and they can save nearly everyting they earn for themselves. Alexa, Silvia and Teresa get two fifty a month and Rosa gets just two hundred, but my cousin gives her thirty pesos a month just to spend, only to spend, because she would save it all and that's not good. She is in charge of the *maquina de lavar,* the washing machine—nothing else. She doesn't have to iron or anything. My cousin has someone come in for that."

I wanted so much to see Rosa in charge of her machine. Rosa who had never been to Merida a year ago, who had been so close to Anita. Her mother can hardly wait to see her in November when she comes home for the fiestas.

"My sisters help with the store and Alexa with the house and they all live in a room together and have so much fun."

"But what about novios, do you have a special one?"

"No, we all have some friends, but so far there has been no trouble. My cousin makes sure we don't go out at night alone. We see boys, but just in groups. I do hope I get to go—to come—soon. But with the new baby and the store at home . . . I wish I could have my turn soon.

"I would like to take a course in Merida, not just work. Maybe I could learn to sew. I could earn more if I went to Can Cum, but I want to spend some time in Merida.

"Or maybe I could go somewhere else—do you remember Berta's sister-in-law, who was living with her? She has gone to Cozumel. I don't know exactly what she's doing. And one of my friends is in Mexico City, working for a relative of my compadre, the doctor from Valladolid. Maybe that would be fun for me; they treat her like a daughter, not a servant.

"My *parientes,* relatives, make it such fun for us. On Sundays they take us to the beaches, to fiestas, to wherever we want to go. He won't let us pay for anything. They want us to *ahorrar,* to save, for ourselves. Why he even bought us pantsuits from Mexico. He went there to a meeting of Alcoholics Anonymous. Do you know that organization? He's an officer, president or something, he goes every year. They treat the girls, all of us like their daughters. They have just two little boys, ten and six. My cousin has her own car. How sad that we can't go by before your plane leaves. Can't you stay?"

But I couldn't. I wished I could.

"I'm writing down their address, the house, the store, it's all the same address and everything. Do call next time. I'm writing down the telephone number and everything, and the bus that goes right by the corner, stops here. Just let me out here, and do write, and do come back."

She waked her little brother, picked up her bag and purse, and I hurried on to catch my plane, furious with myself as always, that I had commitments in Mexico City which could not be changed.

And so, since the road opened in Chan Kom at least eighteen young women have left Chan Kom, according to Felicia, maybe more she says, because now people are leaving all the time.

Eight to Can Cum

Five to Merida (Rosa, Alexa, Silvia, Teresa, Linda)

One to Mexico City

Three to Quintano Roo

One to Cozumel

So in Chan Kom there are only two young unmarried women over thirteen left in the nine households I studied, and one, Felicia, wants to leave. In fact she has made several short trips away—to Merida. She is questioning—as I feel the others are—what she should, must, might do. Not marry . . . not yet . . . but who? nd the others. This certainly spells change for Chan Kom—for both men and women.

Appendix 1

Anita's Budget*

ANITA	COST IN PESOS
5 new huipiles	148.00
4 new fustanas	80.00
1 pair shoes	20.00
1 rebozo	60.00
Total	308.00
DEMETRIO	
3 pair pants	105.00
4 shirts	48.00
2 pair shoes	36.00
	189.00
ROSITA	
3 dresses and 1 huipil	105.00
1 mantilla	15.00
2 pair shoes	50.00
chain	90.00
	260.00
ESPERANZA	
dresses	25.00
shoes	8.00
	33.00
ELENA	
dresses	25.00
shoes	15.00
	40.00

*The clothing purchases are made at the fiesta and are supposed to last for two years.

Food per week	Cost per week (pesos)†
1 carga maize	50.00
2 kilos frijoles	10.00
chili—home grown	
15 eggs	7.50
3/4 chicken	9.00
fruit—rare	1.00
meat—bought in bulk	14.00
sugar—2 kilos	5.00
salt—1 kilo	1.00
chocolate—2 packets	4.50
bread—three purchases	9.00
Total	111.00

Miscellaneous	
lime—1 kilo	.50
molino—.40 per day	2.80
soap—14 soaps	15.00
2 azul—blueing	.50
books, pencils, etc., (15 plus per child)	50.00
wood—gather own	
Total	68.80
	(plus) 111.00
Total weekly expenses	179.80

Anita and Demetrio own four pigs, twenty chickens, eighteen head of cattle (although Humberto says he owns thirty), a jicarilla tree, and chile plants. For additional income, Anita was running a restaurant for five of the men working on the road, each of whom paid seven pesos a day for his three meals.

Originally when I asked Anita how much she spent a week, she wasn't sure because she buys on credit at Eduardo's store. We figured out this budget later on together.

†12.50 pesos per dollar

Appendix 2

One of the reasons for choosing Chan Kom was the abundance of historical and ethnographic material of the Yucateca Maya. I would like to refer first to the material which had been collated by the *Human Relations Area Files.* In checking the *Outline of Cultural Materials* at the Social Relations Department at Harvard, I found that the Yucateca Maya sources were divided into four categories:

NV 1. Aboriginal

NV 2. Historical

NV 3. Before 1610

NV 10. Post-conquest and Modern

There was no material under the first three categories, but under NV 10 the following books and materials were listed and had been coded using the Murdock system:

1. Steggerda, Morris, *Maya Indians of Yucatan,* 1941, Carnegie Institute Washington, Publication 531.
2. Redfield, Robert, and Alfonso Villa Rojas, *Chan Kom, A Maya Village,* 1934, University of Chicago.
3. Redfield, Robert, *A Village That Chose Progress,* 1962, University of Chicago.
4. Villa Rojas, Alfonso, *The Maya of East Central Quintana* R00 - 1945, Carnegie Institute, Washington, Publication 559.
5. Shattuck, George Cheever, *The Peninsula of Yucatan. Medical, Biological, Meteorological and Sociological Studies.* Carnegie Institution of Washington Publication No. 431, Washington, D. C., 1931.
6. Gann, Thomas W. F., *The Maya Indians of Southern Yucatan and Northern British Honduras,* Smithsonian Institution, Bureau of American Ethnology, Bulletin 64. Washington: Government Printing Office, 1918.

7. Thompson, J. Eric S., *The Rise and Fall of the Maya Civilization,* University of Oklahoma Press, Norman, Oklahoma, 1954.

8. Strickon, Arnold, "Hacienda and Plantation in Yucatan: An Historical-Ecological Consideration of the Folk-Urban Continuum in Yucatan." *América Indígena,* Vol. 25, pp. 35–63. Mexico: Instituto Indigenista Interamericano, 1955.

9. Goldkind, Victor. "Social Stratification in the Peasant Community: Redfield's Chan Kom Reinterpreted." *American Anthropologist,* Vol. 67, pp. 863–884. Menasha: Anthropological Association, 1965.

10. Larsen, Helga. "Trip from Chichen-Itza to Xcacal, Q. R., Mexico." *Ethnos,* Vol. 29, pp. 5–42. Stockholm, Sweden: The Ethnographical Museum of Sweden, 1964.

Glossary

actos ceremonies

aguardiente alcohol made from sugar cane

ahatanzhob professional match-maker

ajido god-child

albaniles stone masons

arrepitas sweet cookies

atole corn-meal gruel

baile dance

balche special ceremonial alcoholic drink made from honey

banqueta small stool

barrio neighborhood

bautismo baptism

calabaza wash

caliente (medicina) medicine classified as "hot," no relation to its temperature

casap ik treatment for sickness caused by evil winds, performed by *h-men*

catarro head cold

cenote natural well formed when the limestone surface crust collapses into underground caves

chac-chaac god of water (Mayan); ceremony in honor of the god

chuyub gourd-carriers made of rings of bark

cine movie theatre

cochinas pigs (sows)

codices pre-Columbian illustrated records

codo elbo, stingy (slang)

colonia neighborhood (usually in a city)

comal   round pottery platter on which food is cooked, chiefly tortillas

comerciante   business-person, travelling salesman

comisario   comissioner

comadre   god-mother, by extension, any woman related by such an arrangement

compadre   godfather, by extension, any man related by such an arrangement

curandera   curer, native doctor

de más categoría   more fashionable

dueño   owner, master

ejido   communal land

enchiladas   Mexican dish of filled tortillas with sauce

fagina   free community labor

finados   the dead; also ceremonies honoring them

gallinas   hens

garapatas   chiggers

gorro   cap worn by child during its baptism

granisos   sores on the body

gremio   guild; also used in Chan Kom to refer to the ceremony performed during the fiesta to San Diego, the parade of candles and banners from houses to the church

güero   blonde, fair

habin   a tree

hauncabzil   newlywed man who goes to live with his in-laws

henequen   plant from which fiber is extracted

hetzmek   ceremony for children celebrating their third or fourth month; after this, child is carried astride the left hip

hikab   massage all over the body

h-men   shaman and priest (Mayan)

huipil   traditional dress of Mayan women; loose white poplin shift with embroidered neck and hem

ilibtzil   newlywed woman who goes to live with her in-laws

injecciones   injections, "shots"

jacal   thatched hut

jarana   traditional folk dance

jícara   gourd-like fruit which grows on a tree; bowl made of the gourd

koben   kitchen

kuum   squash

ladino   outsider, non-Indian

lec   pottery bowl used for ceremonies

lenar to gather wood

loh casa ceremony to rid a new house of evil spirits

loh-kex ceremony to appease mountain spirits

machete long, large, heavy knife used to cut underbrush, etc.

maldades witchcraft, calling one bad names, illicit sex, wickedness

mal de ojo evil eye

maestro cantor leader of chants in the church

manta muslin

manzana block (city)

margaritas daisies

masa ground corn which has been soaked in water and lime; dough

mecate twenty square meters of land

me encantaba mucho I liked it very much

mestizo half-breed, usually of mixed Indian and Spanish origins

metate flat stone on which corn is ground

mexiforma medicine for diarrhea

milpa plot of land for growing corn

milpero man who tends a milpa

modista seamstress

molino gristmill

monte literally mountain; used in Yucatan to refer to the bush, out in the country

municipio township

murcielago bat (animal)

muy comadrona a good midwife

muy delicado very touchy; literally, delicate

muy duro very hard; when referring to work carries overtone of importance

muy listo ready, bright, alert

muy satisfecha very satisfied

muy trabajadora hard working, diligent

nana woman (or girl) who cares for one's children

nixtamal gristmill; also *masa* fresh from the mill

novena series of prayers and hymns, including a recitation of a rosary. (In Chan Kom, does not mean nine consecutive evenings of prayer, necessarily)

oficios official documents

olla clay pot

ojo eye

oratorio chapel

pallido pale

palos sticks, poles

papelería paperwork

parcela plot of land

partera midwife

pavos turkeys

Pib earth oven; also refers to a ceremonial meal

porquerías a no no; a naughty act, filthy or dirty words or deeds

pozole corn meal mixed with water; drunk either as a beverage or made into soup

presidente municipal elected village leader

prestado loaned

predio town property

puesto a little store

pura medicina just medicine, nothing more

rancho, ranchería small farm with animals out in the country

ratoncita little mouse

reboza long shawl

regalado made a present of

registro civil town clerk

reglas menstrual periods

relleno negro black stuffing made with special spices

rezoneras women who sing religious chants or prayers

rezos prayers especially recited for the dead

sabucan carrying-bag made of henequen fiber

semana santa holy week (the week before Easter;

sociedad a society; also used to refer to a cooperative

solar a piece of land in town

soltera single woman

soga rope

suciedad dirt, filth, shit

tamales masa, mixed with lard, sometimes filled, wrapped in banana leaves or corn husks, and steamed

tortillas corn meal masa patted into thin round cakes and baked on a hot griddle

un poco de adelante a little bit ahead

vaquera cowgirl; girl friend of a vaquero

vaquero cowboy

verguenza embarrassment, shame

vientos maleficos bad, evil winds

War of the Castes civil war in Yucatan and Quintana Roo which began in 1847, ended in 1858, arising from mistreatment of the Indians by the non-Indians

xamach comal

yerbatero/a one who cures with herbs

yumtzilob Mayan for masters of the mountain, spirit gods

zaca cooked ground corn

zacate stiff fiber

zaz-tun majic stone used like a crystal ball

Bibliography

Avila, Manuel. 1969. *Tradition and Growth: A Study of Four Mexican Villages.* Chicago: The University of Chicago Press

Boserup, Ester. 1970. *Women's Role in Economic Development.* New York: St. Martins Press

Boulding, Elise. 1970. "Women as Role Models in Industrializing Societies: A Macro-System of Socialization for Civic Competence." Boulder: University of Colorado—mimeographed

Brenner, Anita. 1970. *Idols Behind Altars.* U.S.A.: Beacon Press reprint

Camara, Fernando B. 1966. *Persistencia y Cambio Cultural entre Tzeltales de los Altos de Chiapas.* Mexico: INAH

Chinas, Beverly. 1971. "Women as ethnographic subjects." in *Women in Cross-cultural Perspective.* compiled by S. E. Jacobs pp. 21-31. Urbana: University of Illinois

Chinas, Beverly. 1973. *The Isthmus Zapotecs, Women's Roles in Cultural Context.* New York: Holt, Rinehart and Winston.

Collier, Jane Fishburne. 1973. *Law and Social Change in Zinacantan.* Stanford: Stanford University Press

Elmendorf, Mary. 1971. "Role of Women as Agents for Peaceful Social Change." Ottawa: Society for International Development.—mimeographed. (12th World Conference)

———. 1972. *The Mayan Woman and Change.* Cuernavaca, Mexico: CIDOC Cuaderno.

———. 1973. *La Mujer Maya y el Cambio,* Mexico: SEP-sententas

Elu de Lenero, Maria del Carmen. 1969. *Hacia donde va la mujer Mexicana?.* Mexico: Instituto Mexicana de Estudios Sociales, IMES

———. 1971. *Mujeres que Hablan.* Mexico: Instituto Mexicana de Estudios Sociales, IMES

Evans-Pritchard, E. 1965. *The Position of Women in Primitive Societies.* New York: The Free Press

156

Finney, Joseph C. 1969. *Cultural Change, Mental Health, and Poverty.* Lexington: University of Kentucky Press

Freire, Paulo. 1971. *Pedagogy of the Oppressed.* New York: Herder and Herder

Fromm, Erich. 1946. *The Fear of Freedom.* London: Keeger Paul, French, Turner

Fromm, Erich and Michael Maccoby. 1970. *Social Character in a Mexican Village: A Socio-psychoanalytic Study.* Englewood Cliffs, New Jersey: Prentice-Hall

Gann, Thomas W. F. 1918. *The Maya Indians of Southern Yucatan and Northern British Columbia.* Washington, D. C.: Smithsonian Inst., Bureau of American Ethnology, Bulletin 1964, U. S. Government Printing Office

Goldkind, Victor. 1965. "Social Stratification in the Peasant Community: Redfield's Chan Kom Reinterpreted." *American Anthropologist.* Vol. 67: 863-887

Gonzalez N., Moises. 1970. *Raza y tierra.* Mexico: El Colegio de Mexico

Hellbom, Anna-Britta. 1967. *La Participacion Cultural de las Mujeres.* Stockholm: The Ethnographical Museum

Hernandez, D. Juan J. (1849–1943). *Costumbres de las Indias de Yucatan.* Mexico: Boletin del Archivo General de la Nacion, Secretaria ae Gobernacion

Illich, Ivan. 1968. "Outwitting the Developed Countries," Cuernavaca, Mexico: CIDOC Publications

Jacobs, Sue Ellen. 1971. *Women in Cross Cultural Perspective.* Urbana: University of Illinois Press

Kaberry, Phyllis M., (1939)-1973. *Aboriginal Woman.* New York: Gordon Press

Landa, Diego de. 1566. *Relacion de las Cosas de Yucatan.* Madrid: manuscript

Lee, Dorothy. 1955. "Studies of Whole Cultures—Greece," in the *Cultural Patterns and Technical Change.* pp. 57-96. UNESCO: Mentor

———. 1959. *Freedom and Culture.* Englewood Cliffs. New Jersey: Prentice-Hall

Levi-Strauss, Claude. 1972. *(The Savage Mind)* quoted in *Comment,* May 14, 1972, p. 2. U.S.A.: The Merkle Press

Lewis, Oscar. 1969. *Tepotzlan—Village in Mexico.* New York: Holt, Rinehart, and Winston

Lomnitz, Larissa. 1973. "The Survival of the Unfittest". presented at the IXth ICAES, International Congress of Anthropological and Ethnological Sciences: Chicago

———. Oct. 1973. "La Mujer Marginada en Mexico," Mexico: *Dialogos* Magazine

Maccoby, Michael and George M. Foster. 1970. "Methods of Studying Mexican Peasant Personality: Rorschach, TAT and Dreams". *Anthropological Quarterly*. Vol. 43 No. 4 (fall)

Macias, Anna, 1971. "Mexican Women in Social Revolution." American Historical Association, Report of Annual Meeting

Marshall, John. 1970. "Topics and Networks in Intra-Village Communications". University of North Carolina—mimeographed

Mead, Margaret. 1955. *Cultural Patterns and Technical Change*. UNESCO: Mentor Press

Morley, Sylvanus C. and George Brainford. 1956. *The Ancient Maya*. Palo Alto, California: Stanford University Press. Third Edition

Nash, June. 1969. *Social Relations in Amatenango del Valle, an activity analysis*. Mexico: CIDOC

New College. 1972. Report On Intentional Communities. Unpublished-mimeographed. Sarasota, Florida: New College

Park, Robert E. and Ernest W. Burgess. 1921. *Introduction to the Science of Sociology*. Chicago: University of Chicago Press

Paul, Louis. 1974. "The Mastery of Work and the Mystery of Sex: A Highland Maya Case". in *Woman, Culture and Society,* ed. Michelle Z. Rosaldo and Louise Lamphere, Stanford University Press

Redfield, Robert and Alphonso Villa Rojas. 1934. *Chan Kom, A Maya Village.* Washington: Carnegie Institute

Redfield, Robert. 1941. *The Folk Culture of Yucatan*. Chicago: University of Chicago Press

————. 1950. *A Village that Chose Progress: Chan Kom Revisited*. Chicago: University of Chicago Press

————. 1955. *The Little Community*. Chicago: University of Chicago Press

————. 1956. *Peasant Society and Culture*. Chicago: University of Chicago Press

Schwartz, Lola Romanucci. 1962. *Morality, Conflict and Violence in a Mexican Mestizo Village*. PhD Dissertation in Anthropology, University of Indiana (unpublished)

Stavenhagen, Rodolfo. 1966. "Seven Erroneous Theses About Latin America". in *New University Thought,* Vol. 4, #4

Steggerda, Morris, 1941. *Maya Indians of Yucatan*. Washington: Carnegie Publication No. 531

Stevens, Evelyn P. 1973. "Machismo and Marianismo". *Society* periodical. Sept.-Oct. 1973, pp. 57-63

Strickon, Arnold. 1965. *"Hacienda and Plantation in Yucatan."* *América Indígena,* Vol. 25: pp. 35-63. Mexico: Instituto Indigenista Interamericano

Thompson, J. Eric S. 1954. *The Rise and Fall of Maya Civilization*. Norman: University of Oklahoma Press

Tozzer, Alfred M. 1941. Editor of 8th edition of Landa's *Relación de las Cosas de Yucatan.* Papers of the Peabody Museum, Vol. 18. Cambridge: Harvard University

UNESCO. 1964. *A Dictionary of the Social Sciences—1964.* Glencoe: The Free Press

Villa Rojas, Alfonso. 1945. *The Maya of East Central Quintana Roo.* Washington: Carnegie Inst. Pub. # 559.

———. 1969. "The Maya of Yucatan," *Handbook of Middle American Indians,* Vol. 7: pp. 244-272. Austin: University of Texas Pub

Vogt, Even Z. 1969. "The Maya: Introduction," *Handbook of Middle American Indians,* Vol. 7: pp. 21-28. Austin: University of Texas Pub

Wolfe, Eric. 1959. *Sons of the Shaking Earth.* Chicago, London: University of Chicago Press

———. 1966. *Peasants,* Englewood, New Jersey: Prentice-Hall

NINE MAYAN WOMEN

by Mary Elmendorf

Nine Mayan Women describes and analyzes the roles of peasant women in a traditional society faced with the prospect of change in the face of modernization. Focusing on a Mayan village (Chan Kom), Professor Elmendorf characterizes these nine women and discusses their lives, their hopes, and their fears as they strive to adjust to changing social conditions.

The volume is divided into two complementary sections. The opening section presents a series of vignettes couched in the language of the women themselves. The second section includes a statement of the author's primary concerns, a detailed description of the physical, social and political milieu of the village and an analysis of the nature of the women's lives.

Professor Elmendorf emphasizes the human element throughout her study. Especially noteworthy is her perception of her subjects as *women* — women who are concerned with the ways in which they can enhance the quality of life in their community. The author documents the methods by which these women attempt to secure a vital role in the decision-making processes of the village. By making the lives of the peasants its central concern and by raising value-related questions concerning modernization and the role of women, *Nine Mayan Women* challenges readers to form their own judgements about the effects of social change on a traditional peasant society.